THE SPIRAL OF TIME SERIES

RAV DOVBER PINSON

THE MONTH of TISHREI

vol **7**

A TIME OF REBIRTH & UPWARD MOVEMENT

IYYUN PUBLISHING

Published by IYYUN Publishing
232 Bergen Street
Brooklyn, NY 11217

http:/www.iyyun.com

Iyyun Publishing books may be purchased for educational, business or sales promotional use. For information please contact: contact@IYYUN.com

Editor: Reb Matisyahu Brown

Developmental Editor: Reb Eden Pearlstein

Proofreading / Editing: Simcha Finkelstein

Cover and book design: RP Design and Development

Cover image:
by Brin Levinson for The Misaviv Hebrew Circle Calendar by Deuteronomy Press.
www.circlecalendar.com

pb ISBN 978-1-7338130-8-2

Pinson, DovBer 1971-
The Month of Tishrei: A Time of Rebirth and Upward Movement
1.Judaism 2. Jewish Spirituality 3. General Spirituality

vol **7**

THE MONTH
of TISHREI

A TIME OF REBIRTH
& UPWARD MOVEMENT

INCLUDING AN EXPLORATION OF THE
PROGRESSION OF THE HIGH HOLY DAYS

IYYUN PUBLISHING

בס"ד

THE MONTH OF TISHREI

THIS BOOK IS DEDICATED
IN LOVING MEMORY OF

Dr. Allen Gaisin זצ"ל

אליהו בן מנחם מנדל הכהן ז"ל

AN EXCEPTIONAL AND PRECIOUS
INDIVIDUAL

נפטר בשם טוב

י"ח תמוז תשע"ט / July 21, 2019

By his wife Sheila and their children

Miriam, Meredith, Arthur, Daniel,
Jeremy, Reuven and Shlomo.

In honor of his love for Torah,
may the printing of these Torah thoughts
and the inspiration they provide
be an Aliyah for his Neshama!

CONTENTS

CONTENTS

PART II:
Essays on the Yamim Tovim / Holy days of Tishrei

OPENING

*E*ACH MONTH OF THE YEAR RADIATES DISTINCT QUALITIES and provides unique opportunities for personal growth and spiritual illumination. Accordingly, each month has a slightly different climate and represents a particular stage in the "story of the year" as expressed through the annual cycles of nature. The winter months call for practices and pursuits that are different than those of the summer months. Some months are filled with holy days and some have only one or none. Each month therefore has its own natural and spiritual signature.

According to the deeper dimensions of the Torah, each month's distinct qualities, opportunities and natural phenomena correspond to a coordinated set of data arranged within a 12-part symbolic structure. That is, the spiritual nature of each month is articulated according to its unique entries for each of the 12 data points which include: 1) a permutation of G-d's Four-Letter Name, 2) a verse from the Torah, 3) a letter of the Aleph Beis, 4) the name of the month itself, 5) an experiential "sense", 6) a Zodiac sign, 7) a tribe of Israel, 8) a body part, 9) an element, 10) a unit of successive Torah portions that are read during the month, 11) a season of the year, and 12) the holy days that occur during the month.

By reflecting on these twelve themes and categories, an ever-ascending spiral of insight, understanding and practical action becomes revealed. Learning to navigate and harness the nature of change by consciously engaging with the cycles of time adds a deeper sense of purpose and heightened presence to our lives.

The present volume will explore the spiritual nature of the first month of the yearly cycle, the month of Tishrei, according to these 12 categories.

NOTE: For a more comprehensive treatment of this 12-part system and the overarching dynamics of the "story of the year", an in-depth introduction has been provided in Volume One of this series, The Spiral of Time: Unraveling the Yearly Cycle.

ぴ

The Month of Tishrei:

A Time of Rebirth & Upward Movement

CALENDARS ARE SCRIPTS; THEY PROVIDE THE STORYLINE and stage directions for the year based on movements of the earth in relation to other celestial bodies. In the story of terrestrial time there is most often one primary protagonist in relation to the earth: the sun or the moon. Throughout the world, virtually every calendar tells the story of the earth's correspondence with one of these two celestial characters as they chart their path across the sky — every calendar, that is, except for the Hebrew calendar. In our calendar, there are two simultaneous and interlocking stories functioning within the year; we collate and count time by both the solar and lunar cycles. From the lunar cycle we count the months of the year. From the solar cycle, we count the days of the year. Thus, there are two different calendrical 'new years'. The lunar cycle begins with the first *month* of the year, Nisan, while the solar cycle begins with the first *day* of the year, Rosh Hashanah, the first day of Tishrei. In other words, Tishrei starts the new year of the *day*s, Nisan the new year of the *months*.

As explored in the volume on the Month of Nisan, months themselves are connected to the experience of newness and rebirth, as manifest in the monthly renewal of the moon. This is explicitly reflected in the Hebrew words *Chodesh* / month and *Chidush* / renewal. In contrast, years and days are connected to the experience of routine, order, and predictability. This is reflected in the Hebrew word *Shana* / year, which is connected to the word *Yashan* / old. Tishrei is the beginning of the new Shana.

Nisan begins the spring and summer months, and the new year of 'the miraculous'; of redemption, freedom, and revelation from Above. All of this represents a movement from Above to below. Tishrei begins the fall and winter months, and the new year of 'the orderly'; of our own *Avodah* / spiritual-mental-emotional work. This represents a movement from below to Above.

New beginnings are exciting, stimulating a sense of *Hischadshus* / newness, rebirth, hope, possibility, and openness to the unexpected. Regarding such beginnings, Rav Eleazer of Worms (c. 1176-1238), the author Sefer Rokeach, teaches, אין חוזק כחוזק החסידות בתחלתו / (loosely translated) "there is no strength like the strength of a person beginning a new path of *Chassidus* / piety." Rebbe Tzadok of Lublin comments, כי על ידי האור הגדול בוער בלבו חשק ורצון לקדושה בכל תוקף ועוז / "since through this great light, there is aroused in his heart a deep longing and desire for holiness, with tremendous urgency and power" (*Pri Tzadik*, Beshalach). In such a beginning, one senses that abundant "great light" is being opened for him, and his heart and mind are aroused and awakened from their slumber. It feels exciting, fresh and new, much like the visceral sensation when spring arrives after a long, hard, cold winter. This is like the new beginning of Nisan, the month of miracles and our exodus from exile.

And then there is a new beginning of the cycle of the 'old'; the beginning of routine, of inner work and self-elevation, the month of Tishrei. This begins with the inception of the fall and winter months, as the days are getting shorter in the Northern Hemisphere, with less and less sunlight, and increasingly cold temperatures. This beginning demands tenacity, knowing that you are soon going to traverse a long winter, with everything that this absence of light and heat represents.

This beginning of Tishrei and the new year demands introspection, resolution, commitment, and a resolve to persevere. In contrast to the beginning of Nisan, the sages teach regarding the beginning of Tishrei, כל התחלות קשות / "All beginnings are difficult" (*Mechilta*. See Rashi, *Shemos*, 19:5. *Zohar* 2, p. 187). We have to adjust to the new reality and learn to self-generate. Indeed, such beginnings can seem much less exciting and more threatening, awe-inspiring, maybe even harsh and difficult. And yet, this is precisely why the new year begins with the solemn, intensely holy Days of Awe; Rosh Hashanah, the Ten Days of Teshuvah and Yom Kippur. These are not, of course, sad days (G-d forbid), nor should they be filled with stress, anxiety and apprehension. Rather, they are meant to be days of awe, serious introspection, inspiration, and ultimately empowerment.

There is a paradigm of miracles, gifts we receive from Above, which are unexpected or beyond our choice, such as beautiful weather. There is also a paradigm of 'natural causes' and free-choice, in which we ourselves participate and fill in the content of life. Nisan, therefore, embodies the quality of newness in the paradigm of the miraculous, while Tishrei embodies the quality of newness in the paradigm of the natural. Hence, Nisan is connected with the Exodus from Egypt and Tishrei with the Creation of the World. In fact, the Torah opens with the Creation story and the first word of the Torah is בראשית / "In (or with) the beginning..." The word בראשית can be rearranged to spell the words ב- א' תשרי / "In (or with) the first day of Tishrei". In Nisan we celebrate our birth as Klal Yisrael, while in Tishrei we are celebrating the birth of humanity.

Tishrei begins the colder, fall and winter months, and as such, the movement is from below upwards. In the winter months, heat needs to be self-created, both literally and metaphorically. Tishrei is unlike Nisan, a month saturated with *Nisim* / miracles, rather it is the beginning of our 'humanity'. In this way, the focus of Tishrei is on our commitment to the Creation and taking upon ourselves new resolutions as well as taking responsibility for how we are creating our own day-to-day lives

FROM ELUL TO TISHREI

The month before Tishrei is Elul. In Elul we concluded the past year, gathered it in like a deep inhale, owned it and dealt with it. Elul is a month of *Teshuvah* / returning 'from' negativity and returning 'to' Hashem. We examine and let go of old negative behaviors, moving from remorse to acceptance, and then to self-illumination. Now, as Tishrei enters, we 'exhale', so-to-speak, into the new year as we blow the Shofar. While Elul is a time for gathering up the entire past year as it ends, Tishrei is a time for projecting a good incoming year and a fresh new beginning.

In the process of Teshuvah, 'returning' to alignment with our deepest selves, there are two essential stages: first, *Charata*/regretting and contemplating the past, and second, *Kabbalah*/acceptance and creating resolutions and solutions for the future. First we must break away from our old life, and then we can begin a new life. Elul is about owning our shortcomings and breaking away from perpetuating them, and Tishrei is the new beginning, the rebirth.

Only once Teshuvah is established in a person, with sincere regret and resolve, can they consciously receive forgiveness. This is true not only of forgiveness from Heaven, but if we have acted negatively toward others, or even if we have let ourselves down, Teshuvah allows us to receive forgiveness from others, and to truly forgive ourselves. Elul is the deep reservoir of Teshuvah. Tishrei is the fountain of forgiveness that flows from that very place. The peak of forgiveness is crowned with Yom Kippur, the day of total Divine forgiveness and atonement.

PERMUTATION OF HASHEM'S NAME

THE FOUR-LETTER ESSENTIAL NAME, YUD-HEI-VAV-HEI (known as *Hashem* / the Name), is the Divine Source of all Reality. The last three letters of the Name, Hei-Vav-Hei, create the word *Hoveh* / 'is', the present. The root of this verb means, 'to bring into being'. The first letter of the Name, Yud, serves as a prefix to the last three letters: *Yud-HoVeH*. In this way, the Yud modifies the verb to represent a perpetual activity. In other words, the Divine Name can be understood to mean, 'That Which Is Continuously Bringing Being Into Being'.

For numerous reasons, this Essential Name cannot be spoken. Therefore a common practice is to rearrange its four letters into an alternate construction that may be pronounced. This produces the word *HaVaYaH*, which literally means 'Being-ness'. This aspect of the Name refers to the Ultimate Being, which is the Source and Substance of all that is. The Ultimate Being does not depend on anything else to exist. It gives rise to all past, present and future manifestations, thereby bringing all things into existence ex nihilo, i.e. *Yesh meAyin* / being from non-being. Accordingly, the individual words for 'was' / *Hayah*, 'is' / *Hoveh*, and 'will be' / *Yihyeh*, are all encoded within the Essential Name.

Since the Four-Letter Name is the Source of all Being and Time, it is inherently connected to actual time. Because of this, each unique period in time is imbued with a special connection to the Name. This connection is expressed through a unique permutation of the four letters that comprise the Name, an inner light that 'shines' through the 'prism' of each permutation. Each permutation communicates a different spiritual dynamic which is part of the Divine signature encoded within that particular month.

The sequence of the four letters in Hashem's name which corresponds to the month of Tishrei is Vav-Hei-Yud-Hei.*

---

* The vowels in the sequence of Hashem's name for the month of Tishrei are Vav with a Patach, Hei with a Cholam, Yud with a Kamatz, and Hei with a Patach. The words' final letters, from which the sequence is derived, have different vowels beneath them (ויראו שרי אתה פרעה / *VayirU osO sareI PharaoH* / "The princes of Egypt saw"), however, the *Tikunei Zohar* (Hakdamah, 2b) explains that we use the first letters for the *Nekudos* of a sequence of Hashem's name.

Examining these four letters more closely, the ו / Vav and י / Yud, are a line and a dot respectively, representing a masculine quality. The open letter ה / Hei represents a feminine quality. Within the Name, Yud-Hei is the higher configuration of masculine and feminine, and Vav-Hei is the lower configuration. The letter sequence of the month of Tishrei begins with the lower masculine-feminine dynamic (Vav-Hei) and ends with the higher masculine-feminine dynamic (Yud-Hei). This sequence describes an upward movement of אתערותא דלתתא / *Isarusa d'le Tata* / 'awakening from below' and elevation from 'the below' upward. This movement is in contrast to the sequence of the first *Chodesh* / month of the year, the month of Nisan, when the higher masculine-feminine dynamic precedes the lower one, representing an אתערותא דלעילא / *Isarusa d'le'Eila* / 'awakening from Above'.

Tishrei is all about 'the below', the creation of humanity, the judgment of humanity, the natural world, and the beginning of the new year of the days, which is human 'routine'.

When this sequence of letters, Vav-Hei-Yud-Hei, is read as a word it spells והיה / *v'Hayah* / 'and it shall come to pass.' Our sages tell us that the word *v'Hayah* is a term expressing joy, suggesting that something positive is going to happen in the following verses. The word ויהי / *vaYehi* / 'and it was,' however, is a term expressing hardship, implying that something ominous or sad is about to occur (*Megilah*, 10b).

Perhaps this is related to onomatopoeia: *v'Hayah* sounds like a shout of joy, while *vaYehi* sounds like a *Kvetch* / complaint of 'Oy-vey' (Note: *Midrash Rabbah*, Beshalach). Thus *vaYehi* is understood to indicate the presence of *Tza'ar* / hardship, whereas *v'Hayah* indicates the presence of Simchah / joy.

ויהי / *vaYehi* without the Vav is יהי / *Yehi* / 'it shall be', future tense. When the Vav is added as a prefix, it transforms the word from future tense to past tense: 'And it was.' The future becomes the past. The opposite is true for the word *v'Hayah* / 'And it shall come to pass,' future tense. Without the Vav it spells היה / *Hayah* / 'it was,' past tense. The prefix of Vav makes the past become the future (Gra, *Aderes Eliyahu*, Bereishis, 1:3).

Frustrations, pinings and yearnings are for the future. Sadness is about the past. People are not sad for things they never had, rather they become saddened when loved ones or things in their lives have become lost or 'past tense.' When a person looks back and says, 'Those were the good old days,' they live with sadness; the best of life seems to be forever gone. And so, *vaYehi*, "and it was", is a term of sadness. When a person's 'future' is all in the past, when they live without hope for a brighter future, they live with sadness and despair. By contrast, when something is already in the past, but then it becomes available again in the future, it brings joy; when the 'past' becomes the 'future' there is Simchah. Where there is a future there is joy. When we assume the posture of *v'Hayah* / "and it shall come to pass", we can live with hope, openness and a sense of possibility for the future. Our lives become filled with optimism and joy.

While *Haya* is the past, *v'Hayah* indicates the future. So, *v'Hayah* is a kind of middle place, the present as it moves from the paradigm of the past toward the future. Whereas *Yehi* is the future, *vaYehi* is the past. It is the present moment moving from the future toward the past. These are two ways of experiencing life — either the present is birthed by the past, or it is pulled by a future. To live with joy is to live with hope, future and possibility; a life pulled by the infinite possibilities of the future.

And so, Tishrei calls us to be in the present moment while joyfully expecting a brighter future. The past year may not have been so wonderful — it might even have been excruciating. But with a heart full of hope we can pronounce this traditional blessing for Rosh Hashanah: "May the past year and its curses come to an end! May the New Year and its blessings now begin!"

From this we can begin to understand what is the 'awe' in these 'Days of Awe': It is the awesome sense of both the responsibility and opportunity to start over and create a new beginning, to truly live a life of joy, optimism, meaning and purpose.

ॐ

TORAH VERSE

HE FOUR LETTER PERMUTATION OF THE DIVINE NAME that shines during each month is rooted within a particular verse in the Torah (*Tikunei Zohar, Hakdamah* 9b. *Eitz Chayim, Sha'ar* 44:7). In other words, there is a 'verse of the month' consisting of a four-word sequence, in which each word either begins or ends with the letters of the *Tziruf* / name formation for that month. In fact, the order of the Tziruf follows the corresponding verses (*Mishnas Chasidim*, Meseches Adar, 1:3). The meaning and context of the verse connected with each particular month is, of course, also part of the revelation of that month's guiding light.

The permutation of the Divine Name of this month, the sequence of these four letters of the Name of Hashem, is rooted in the last letters of this month's verse: **ויראו אתה שרי פרעה** / *Vayi-rU osO sareI PharaoH* / "The princes of Egypt saw (Sarah)" (*Bere-ishis*, 12:15). Avraham and Sarah needed to leave the Land of Israel to travel to Egypt because of the famine. And when the princes of Egypt saw Sarah, the wife of Avraham, they desired that she become a wife of Pharaoh because "they saw that she was very beautiful" (*Ibid*, 12:14). Indeed, Sarah was one of the four most beautiful women in the world (*Megilah*, 14a). These verses describe a negatively-charged desire for physical intimacy, one that is based solely on visual infatuation and lust.

Tishrei is a month of rectifying and creating a Tikkun for 'negative' or unholy intimacy and transforming it into holy intimacy, as will be explored. It is also a month that gives us the *Koach* / power to be in the present moment. This power allows us to be truly intimate with people as well as with the 'now' — these two abilities are completely interconnected.

There are two very different ways of 'being in the now'. One is living *for* the now, and the other is living *in* the now. The princes of Egypt were living *for* the now and impulsively desired to be-hold Sarah and bring her to Pharaoh. Their view of the 'now' was cut off from a real past: Sarah was already married. It was also cut off from a real future: they had no intentions of commitment, and they would soon find yet another woman to bring to Pharaoh. This represents 'intimacy' that is cut off from the truth of the living present. Living *for* the now—without intentionality, openness, awareness, or responsibility — limits us to a cut off 'now'. This is not authentic 'presence' and it distorts our relationship with the source and outcome of our actions.

To live *in* the now, however, is to behold the eternal present, which encompasses all of the past, present and future. The real 'now' is not cut off from, but rather in direct contact with the past. As a result, it is also in direct contact with the future outcome of actions taken in the present. When we are living intimately *in* the now, our intimate lives can be that much more wholesome and real, because then there is nothing else, and certainly nobody else, G-d forbid, on our mind besides the other.

In Tishrei, when time begins anew, we are afforded the ability to create a Tikkun for those moments we squandered in living impulsively *for* the now. We can begin to live with deeper presence and attain holy physical intimacy with our spouse, and appropriate emotional and spiritual intimacy with others and with all of life.

LETTER

HERE ARE 22 LETTERS IN THE ALEPH BEIS. THE TORAH, which is the 'Blueprint of Creation', is written in Hebrew, the *Lashon haKodesh* / Holy Tongue, as our sages teach that each of these letters contain a host of metaphysical energies and Divine creative potentials. According to the Sefer Yetzirah, a profound book of early Kabbalah that pays particular attention to the inner dimensions of the Hebrew letters, the 22 letters are divided into three categories: three "Mother Letters", seven "Double Letters" and 12 "Simple Letters." Each month is connected to one of the 12 Simple Letters.*

---

* For a more in-depth analysis of all three categories of Hebrew letters and their relationship to the calendar, please see the introductory volume in this series, *The Spiral of Time: Unraveling the Yearly Cycle.*

The letter associated with the month of Tishrei is Lamed / ל. The graphic design of Lamed looks like two partially delineated triangular spaces: a larger one below and a smaller one above. These two triangles balance each other, like a scale, alluding to Libra, the astrological sign of the month. The scale also alludes to the balanced state of awareness of 'living in the moment', which helps us move toward fulfillment in the future with a sense of responsibility and joy.

Noticeably, the shape of the Lamed also suggests leaping upward, aspiring for more, and reaching higher. It is the only letter in the Aleph-Beis whose peak rises above the upper boundary of the other letters. Throughout Tishrei we rise upward into the world of forgiveness and spiritual elevation, an elevation from the below to the Above.

In Tishrei we are given the ability to start over again. Tishrei is a time to elevate ourselves and leap upwards as we move into the six winter months, characterized by a need to generate our own warmth, which too is a movement 'from below to Above'.

The word *Lamed* actually means *Limud*, 'learning' or 'teaching', alluding to the desire to rise in knowledge. In the Book of Judges, a verse says, "And they smote the *P'lishtim* / Philistines with a מלמד הבקר / *Melamed haBakar* / cattle prod, literally 'a teacher of the cattle' (*Shoftim*, 3:31). We learn from this reference that Lamed is like a *Melamed* / teacher or guide — one that 'prods' us to stay focused on where we are going, where we really want to direct our life. This is one of the functions of the 'new beginning' we are given in Tishrei. The *Yamim Nora'im* / 'Days of Awe' prod us to accelerate toward fulfilling our life's purpose. It teaches us to focus and stay on the path of justice and righteousness.

Beyond conventional teaching and guiding, the Lamed 'points' us to a higher, deeper wisdom. The Zohar calls the letter Lamed מגדל הפורח באויר / "a tower flying through the air" (*Zohar*, 2:91a. See also *Sanhedrin* 106b, Rashi ad loc). This is because the letter Lamed soars above the text line. *Lamed* is a type of learning that soars. There is a type of learning that delves deeply into a subject in an attempt to gain information and understanding of 'what is'. And then there is a type of learning that is imaginative and intuitive, soaring upward beyond information or utilitarian understanding, to 'what could be'. This is the Lamed.

Lamed is spelled ל-מ-ד / Lamed, Mem, Dalet. These three letters are an acronym for the phrase לב מבין דעת / a heart that understands *Da'as* / knowledge (*Osyos d'Rabbi Akiva*, Lamed). Da'as is not merely an intellectual knowing, it is a higher awareness of reality, and a way of living in the present while also aspiring for higher and deeper states of consciousness. אין דעה אלא רוח הקדש / "There is no *Dei'eh* (Da'as) but *Ruach haKodesh* / holy spirit of wisdom" (*Mechilta*, Shemos, 15:20). Da'as is a higher form of knowing, the knowing of the heart which is 'above the line', or above linear thought. This is the letter Lamed.

Lamed, the letter of Tishrei, when combined with the letter of the previous month, the Yud of Elul, produces the word *Li* / 'to me' or mine. In Tishrei Hashem is telling us, 'You are Mine.' During Elul we move 'toward' Hashem so-to-speak, as the letters of the word Elul spell the phrase *Ani L'dodi*, 'I belong to my Beloved....'

However, through the atonement or 'at-one-ment' of Yom Kippur, we receive the Divine response: 'Yes, and you belong to Me!' We then become consciously 'at one' with our Beloved.

The word *Li* has a numerical value of 40 (Lamed = 30, Yud = 10), referring to the 40 days from the First of Elul through the Tenth of Tishrei, which is Yom Kippur. Yom Kippur is the day of our 'marriage' to HaKadosh Baruch Hu, as our sages tell us, ביום חתונתו, זה מתן תורה / "'On the day of his wedding' — this is the giving of the Torah" (*Ta'anis*, 26b) and as Rashi notes, זה מתן תורה, יום הכפורים / "'This is the giving of the Torah' — this is Yom Kippur (the receiving of the Second Tablets)." In the act of marrying a bride, the groom says to her, הרי את מקודשת לי / "You are hereby betrothed *Li* / to me" (*Kiddushin*, 5b). At the culmination of these forty days, this is the declaration that rings forth; we are betrothed, and even married, to HaKadosh Baruch Hu.

During the month of Tishrei we re-affirm and deepen our relationship with HaKadosh Baruch Hu, both as our beloved 'spouse', and paradoxically *Avinu* / our Father, our loving parent who is also *Malkeinu* / our King. The cry of the Shofar is thus either the call of a lover to a beloved to reconnect or an estranged child reaching out to parent — but it is also the sound of a trumpet declaring the anointing of the King, revealing the sovereignty of the Master of the Universe.

Lamed stands at the very center of the Aleph-Beis; there are eleven letters before it and ten after. Lamed is like the King of the letters, standing tall above all the surrounding letters. The letter before Lamed is Kaf, כ , which stands for כסא / *Kisei*, a 'throne', as such, the Medrash tells us that Lamed is a King who sits upon the throne (*Osyos D'Rabbi Akiva*, Lamed). The letter after Lamed is Mem. Together, Kaf, Lamed and Mem form the word מלך / king, with Lamed being the center letter of the word (Maharal on *Avos* 6:6). Correspondingly, Tishrei is the Seventh Month, the 'middle' of the year of months, when we coronate HaKadosh Baruch Hu as the King and Center of the Universe.

During the first ten days of Tishrei, there is a period of *Binyan haMalchus* / 'building up the Divine Kingship'. In other words, our spiritual work elevates the Divine status, so-to-speak, as "there is no king without subjects." Our commitment and work 'allows' the Divine Presence to reign supreme throughout the world. This is another reason why the letter of the month is Lamed. As a kingly letter, Lamed empowers us to rise to our ability to crown Hashem as the King and Master of the World.

Lamed, as mentioned, is numerically 30. The Mishnah says that מלכות נקנית בשלשים מעלות / "Royalty is acquired along with 30 prerogatives" (*Avos*, 6:6). In fact, the first 'Jew' to become an actual 'king' (or vizier) was Yoseph, the son of Yaakov. Yoseph became the leader of Egypt when he was 30 years old (and Yoseph's tribe includes the tribe of Ephrayim, the tribe of this month). The individual who most personifies kingship is King David, as the Rambam writes, עקר המלכות לדוד / "the essential monarchy belongs to David" (*Hilchos Melachim*, 1:8). Appropriately, David became king at the age of 30. During the 30 days of Tishrei we work on crowning HaKadosh Baruch Hu as the King over all of Creation.

NAME OF THE MONTH

ACCORDING TO THE TORAH, NAMES ARE VERY powerful (*Yuma*, 83b. *Tanchuma*, Hazinu. *Berachos*, 7b). Composed as they are of Hebrew letters, names represent and define the energy or attributes of that which is named (*Tanya*, Sha'ar haYichud ve-haEmunah, 1). Our names unlock and reveal hidden potentials present within our own spiritual makeup. Similarly, the names of places and periods of time provide subtle hints as to their deeper purpose or poetic significance. Additionally, changing one's name is akin to a kind of rebirth; some even say that a change of name initiates a change of *Mazal* (Rashi, *Bereishis*, 15:5. *Rosh Hashanah*, 16b. *Yerushalmi*, Shabbos, 6:39. Rama, *Yoreh Deah*, 335:10).

Each of the twelve months of the year has a distinct name, and every name has a meaning. According to our Sages, the current names we have for the months were imported to our tradition upon our return to Israel from the Babylonian Exile (They can in fact be traced to ancient Babylonian or Akkadian names. See *Yerushalmi*, Rosh Hashanah, 1:2. *Medrash Rabbah*, Bereishis, 48:9. Tosefos, *Rosh Hashanah*, 7a. Even Ezra, *Chezkuni*, Shemos, 12:2). In the times before the Babylonian Exile, the names of the months were mostly known by their number in the sequence of the year. For example, the month of Av was called the Fifth Month, Cheshvan was known as the Eighth Month, and Tishrei is simply known as the Seventh Month.

There are, however, a few months of the year that are named in Tanach, in post-Babylonian Exile writings: Nisan is mentioned in the *Megilah* / Scroll of Esther (*Megilas Esther*, 8:9), along with Adar (*ibid*, 3:7), and Teves (*ibid*, 2:16) Nisan, Elul and Kislev are mentioned in the book of *Nechemiyah* (1:1, 2:1).

Prior to the Babylonian Exile, besides being called in the Torah the Seventh Month, Tishrei was also called *Yerech Eisonim* or simply *Eisonim* / 'Month of the Strong Ones' or 'Month of the Ancients' (*Melachim* 1, 8:2), both translations referring to the birth of the Avos, the Patriarchs, who were each born during this month (*Rosh Hashanah*, 11a). After the Babylonian Exile, the month was known as 'Tishrei'.

The name *Tishrei* seems to originate in the Akkadian name of the month, *Tashritu*, meaning in Akkadian 'to begin' or 'to dedicate', since this month was and is the beginning of the agricultural year for all peoples' cultures living in the Western Hemisphere.

Incidentally, the phonetic sound *Tashritu* is very similar to the word *Tari'u* / to blow, a form of the word *Teruah* / Shofar blast, which is a most important word with regards to Rosh Hashanah. The Torah actually calls Rosh Hashanah *Yom Teruah* / a day of Shofar blowing.

Perhaps because Aramaic is similar to Akkadian, the Targum Onkelos uses the word *Tishrei* to mean 'You shall begin' (*Targum* on Devarim, 16:9). Tishrei is the world of beginnings.

The letters of the word *Tishrei,* י ר ש ת (Tav, Shin, Reish, Yud), are the four fundamental letters in the Hebrew word ראשית / beginning (the letter Aleph is just added as a vowel). In fact, the Torah calls the month of Tishrei the רשית השנה / the beginning of the year (*Devarim,* 11:12), and the word רשית is literally the same four letters as the word תשרי in a different sequence.

In Aramaic, says the Kol Bo, the word *Tishrei* also means 'forgiveness'. In the Medrash Tishrei means to 'unbind' or release. Regarding this seventh month, the Medrash says, we ask Hashem to תשרי ותשבוק ותכפר על חובי עמך / "*Tishrei* / unbind, let go and forgive the liabilities of Your People" (*Vayikra Rabba,* 29:8). Tishrei is a time of cosmic forgiveness and an opportune time for us to unbind ourselves from all negativity and stuckness. As we begin a new year, we need to release our past and dedicate ourselves to a positive future. Tishrei gives us the strength to do so.

THE BACKWARD LETTER SEQUENCE

Rosh Hashanah and Yom Kippur are both called "the Days of Judgment", referring to an extremely positive judgment — the verdict being that we will live a good life in the coming year. But the experience is of *Din* / judgment nonetheless. As previously mentioned, the letters spelling the word *Tishrei* move backwards through the Aleph-Beis. The Zohar writes that when the Aleph-Beis is written in a backward direction it represents Din and *Gevurah* / strength (*Zohar* 2, 186a. "Backwards is the secret of Gevurah": *Zohar* 2, 52a).*

Also, backwards progression in this case is synonymous with moving from below upward, as in 'traveling upstream'. As such, our *Avodah* / spiritual-mental-emotional work in Tishrei is to swim upstream toward our Creator and create momentum for rising higher and higher throughout the coming year.

---

* The letters spelling the word *Tishrei* move backwards through the Aleph-Beis: from the final letter backwards. This movement represents *Din* / judgment. The movement from Aleph forward represents *Chesed* / kindness: *Zohar*, 2, 186a. There is an argument in the Gemara whether the world was created in Nisan or Tishrei: *Rosh Hashanah*, 10b. Nisan is a time of miracles, a time of movement from Above to below, and thus the Torah name for Nisan is Aviv, beginning with an Aleph, then a Beis. Tishrei the movement is from below to Above, and thus the letters move backward from Tav to Shin to Reish to Yud. A world created in Nisan is a world that begins with an Aleph, a world of Chesed. A world created in Tishrei is a world that begins with a Tav, a world of Din. The Medrash teaches that the world is created with both judgment and compassion. The first words of the Torah are *Bereishis Bara Elokim Es* / "In the beginning G-d created *Es* / the...." The word *Es* contains the letters Aleph and Tav, implying that the world is founded on both a movement of Chesed / Aleph and a movement of Din / Tav.

Rebbe Eliezer and Rebbe Yehoshua, the great sages of the Mishnah, debate together on when the world (time / space) was created (although it turns out the question is really about when mankind was created). Rebbe Eliezer's opinion is that the Creation took place on the first day of the month of Tishrei, whereas Rebbe Yehoshua asserts that it was on the first day of the month of Nisan (*Rosh Hashanah*, 11a)*.

This is more than a literal question, rather it is a deep philosophical question: In what spiritual and existential paradigm is Creation in general, and the human being in particular, birthed? Who are we at our root?

Nisan is the month of miracles while Tishrei is the 'backward' flow of the letters, the paradigm of rising up and taking responsibility for our lives. What is the nature of the foundation of the world — does it have the qualities of Tishrei, human responsibility, effort and self-elevation, or the quality of Nisan, Divine miracles and simple, humble faith? While both are true, ultimately we

---

* All, however, agree that Tishrei is the seventh month of the year, and in this way, within the context of months, it is the middle month of the year. Whereas Nisan is the 'head' or 'top' of the lunar cycle, Tishrei can then be likened to the 'heart' or 'stomach' of the year, or the place of the womb, of potential for birthing a new year-structure. The debate between Rebbe Eliezer and Rebbe Yehoshua is whether the world is created from the head, or from the heart / stomach / womb. This is an argument regarding the world of *Shanah* / time, and similar debates are found regarding the worlds of *Nefesh* / Soul and *Makom* / Space. Regarding the world of *Nefesh* / soul, human beings, Chazal debate on where we consider the fetus to be created — from the top or 'head', or the middle, the naval area (הולד נוצר מטיבורו או מראשו נברא *Sotah*, 45b). In the world of *Olam* / space, Chazal also debate on where the world was created, from the sides (beginning) of space, or from the middle, the center of space (עולם מאמציעתו נברא או עולם מן הצדדין נברא *Yumah*, 54b).

consider the First of Tishrei to be the Sixth Day of Creation when Adam and Chavah were created; the beginning of the world, from a 'human' standpoint. We are birthed into a condition of responsibility; this is who we are. To be fully human is to take responsibility for your life, to participate and be an active partner in your life's unfolding.

THE NATURAL FLOW OF *Klal* TO *Prat*,
AND ITS REVERSAL

Besides representing the movement from below to Above and the taking of responsibility for life, a backward flow of the Aleph-Beis also represents a movement from *Peratim* / details into a *Klal* / general principle.

Aleph is 1, Beis is 2, and the final letter, Tav, is 400. In this way, Aleph represents the *Klal* / single general principle of existence, which is multiplied into *Peratim* / details as it descends into our world, without losing its character of singularity. In this way, Beis is really two Alephs, and Tav is four hundred Alephs (*Toldos Yaakov Yoseph*, Bereishis. *Toldas Aaron*, Likutim, p. 493).

Inwardly, the Klal represents the state of unity that we have when we are aware of the Ultimate Oneness. This state is called *Gadlus* / expansiveness or 'big mind'. The movement from Klal to Perat is the revealing of Hashem's Oneness, the Aleph within the (apparent) duality and multiplicity of Creation, of time-space-consciousness. The movement of Tishrei is in the opposite direction, referred to as *Ohr Chozer* / reflective light. It is characterized by the Avodah of Teshuvah, a movement in which we gather and elevate all the Peratim of our life and the life around us to the awareness of *Hashem Echad* / the Klal of All Existence is One.

TORAH, *Ohr Yashar*, IS FATHER TO CHILD — TESHUVAH, *Ohr Chozer*, IS CHILD TO FATHER

As mentioned, the sequence of the letters in the name of the month are in reverse order, moving from the last letter of the Alef-Beis toward the first letter. Aleph indicates the first expression of the Infinite Formlessness, while Tav indicates the final manifestation in this world. In Tishrei we move from the 'form' of our lives to the Formless potential. This is termed *Ohr Chozer* / reflective or 'returning' light, and the Path of *Teshuvah* / 'returning' to awareness of the Formless Oneness, where we can recalibrate and readjust our form.

Torah, 'revelation', is *Ohr Yashar* / direct light, moving downward, revealing from Above to below, while *Teshuvah* / 'turning back', is *Ohr Chozer* / reflecting light, moving upward.

There is a path of Torah or 'revelation', which begins in the first month of the year, Nisan, the time of the Redemption from Egypt. This path culminates in the third month of the year, Sivan, the month of the giving of the Torah, with the giving of the first set of *Luchos* / Tablets. This is a movement of Divine Light from Above to below, from Infinite to finitude, from formlessness to form, a refraction of the One into the many and Unity into duality. With this great revelation from Above, we humans below are thrust out of *Mitzrayim* / Egypt, a place of *Meitzarim* / limitations and constrictions. Because of the magnitude of this revelation, all concealments are eclipsed, illuminating all darkness and we are suddenly in a state of expansion and redemption. A mere 50 days since leaving Egypt, we find ourselves standing at Mount Sinai, receiving the grand, overwhelming revelation of Torah. The light of Torah is so intense that we literally expire from finite consciousness and corporeality (*Shabbos*, 88b); all of 'earthly' existence is eclipsed. This is the path of *Ohr Yashar* / direct light moving 'from Aleph to Tav', like a floodlight that illuminates the darkness.

There is also a path of Teshuvah. Here one begins not with Gadlus and Supernal illumination, but rather with *Katnus* / smallness: the humble acknowledgment of one's sin, dissention, falling, brokenness, concealment or estrangement. From the depths of this sensitization to darkness, one feels an urge to change, to get up, to instigate an inner revolution, to feel elevated and light. This movement is from below, *mi-Ma'amakim* / "from the depths". From a heart of darkness and frustration, one cries out for change. One yearns and finds the *Gevurah* / strength to reach upwards and inwards to a glimmer of light, of real joy; with a bolt of energy, one races upstream to a place of *Mer'chav* / expansiveness and oneness.

This is the path of Teshuvah, from the lowest of the low to the highest of the high. Such a transformation is possible because Ohr Chozer can generate a light that is even more intense than that which is revealed from Above. This is similar to a magnifying glass or parabolic reflector, which can gather a 'small' ray of sunlight and contract it upon an object with such focus that fire can leap up.

On Yom Kippur we celebrate the Giving of the Torah a second

time, as on this day we receive the second set of Luchos (*Ta'anis,* 26b. *Rashi,* ad loc). The first set of Luchos was given following the revealing of the Torah which began in the month of Sivan. These Luchos were eventually broken. On a deeper level, this express-es the fact that the First Luchos, the Handiwork of Hashem, descended from On High into a place of brokenness, of darkness and forgetfulness. Perfect wholeness and unity beamed down into a place of separation and fragmentation. In contrast, the Sec-ond Luchos, the handiwork of man, was brought about through Teshuvah, through fixing brokenness and sin — and in this way these Luchos remained, and always remain, complete and whole. The unity that comes from a place of forgetfulness and darkness is Ohr Chozer, light emitted from this dense physical world. Making sincere Teshuvah after a fall, and healing our own brokenness, can create a kind of wholeness and light that can never be broken or dimmed.

Regarding the Torah which is revealed from Above, the Mitzvah is "You shall teach your children" (*Devarim,* 11:19). יודע לדבר אביו לומדו תורה / "If the child knows how to speak, his father teach-es him Torah" (*Sukkah,* 42a). It is a father-to-son dynamic. The Torah is given from our Father in Heaven to us, as it were, and from us parents and teachers to our children and students. Thus the flow from Above to below is perpetuated on all levels. Even by sharing a *Devar Torah* / word of teaching or inspiration with a friend, you are participating in the ongoing downflow of Ohr Yashar.

With regards to Teshuvah, the movement is *Mamash* / literally the opposite. The prophet Malachi says, speaking of Eliyahu haNavi coming to usher in a time of Teshuvah before the Ultimate Redemption: והשיב לב־אבות על־בנים ולב בנים על־אבותם / "He shall return the heart of parents to (their) children and the heart of children to their parents" (*Malachi*, 3:24). This also means והשיב לב־ אבות על־בנים: ע"י בנים / He will cause a return of parents to Hashem 'by means of children' (Rashi, *ad loc*). This is a son-to-father dynamic. This is the 'reverse flow' of Teshuvah: when children inspire their parents to do Teshuvah, the receiver 'below' becomes a giver and influences those who are normally 'above' them. This can be said of our times, when tens of thousands of a younger generation are inspiring their elders and parents to think more seriously about their Yiddishkeit and inspiring them to Teshuvah. This is the overarching theme of Tishrei, the movement from Hashem's children below, reaching upwards toward our Divine Parent. It is an upflow from the natural world toward the higher worlds, from multiplicity to Unity, from *Toldos* / derivatives ('generations') to *Avos* / principals ('parents').

THE BELOW

Taking a closer look at the High Holy Days of Rosh Hashanah and Yom Kippur, one notices that nothing 'miraculous' occurred on these days. In fact, we are not commemorating any specific supernatural events on them. We are not celebrating a Splitting of the Sea, for example, nor a salvation of our people from annihilation. What are we celebrating? We are celebrating our inherent birthright and our ability to reclaim it.

This is diametrically the opposite to Pesach, the time of our redemption from slavery in Egypt, and even Shavuos when we received the Torah. On the High Holidays we celebrate the creation of the world, the birthday of humanity, and an opportunity to be co-creative and realign ourselves with the Supernal Will. These are powerful times indeed, but not by definition 'miraculous'.

Rosh Hashanah and Yom Kippur proclaim unequivocally that our stories, our struggles, our commitments and our strivings all have value. Our life has worth. Rosh Hashanah is our birthday; we celebrate our birth — we celebrate our pure essence, our true self and our purpose in life. We celebrate the fact that we want to live another year, that we are choosing to 'write' ourselves, so-to-speak, into the Book of Life. Yom Kippur is the day we take full responsibility for all of our humanity. It is a *Yom Tov* / Holy Day, on which we celebrate our atonement and our ability to reclaim our inherent birthright.

We are celebrating that we, finite creatures, can rise upward to the highest heights. Instead of the *Shefa* / flow streaming to us from Above, we are creating the flow, we are generating the light, we are directing ourselves back to our Source.

Nissan is the month in which we are given a gift: the Divine Presence miraculously lifts us up and out of our constrictions and entrapments. During this time, we were liberated from *Mitzrayim* / Egypt, both literally and figuratively. *Mitzrayim* is a metaphor for all of our *Meitzarim* / inner constrictions and limitations. In this liberation, the sea splits, both literally and inwardly, and our inner visions became revealed on the external level. And yet, because of this miraculous dynamic, Nissan is not a time where *we learn* how to 'become free'; we are given freedom as a gift. Tishrei, however, is the time when we move upward, of our own volition, from the bottom-up. Tishrei is the time when we decide that we want the connection, and we do whatever it takes to make it. Nissan teaches us how to depend on the Above, while Tishrei teaches us how to motivate and depend on ourselves for our spiritual, mental and emotional growth and refinement.

In Nissan we celebrate *Chodesh haAviv* / the Month of Spring, in which the earth sprouts forth with life, independent of our *Avodah* / spiritual or physical work. Sukkos, by contrast, is called *Chag haAsif* / the Festival of Gathering, celebrating the gathering of the produce from the field, which requires much intense work.

All of Tishrei is characterized by this idea of 'producing' change within ourselves and working to 'gather' it in or integrate it. We participate in a process of self-refinement; we do not passively receive the product. This is why the month of Tishrei is symbolized by the image of scales of judgment (Libra), the idea of balance. True balance is achieved when we are able to receive inspiration from Above or from outside ourselves (as in the month of Nisan), but then to couple that 'inspiration' with 'perspiration'(as in the month of Tishrei) . This drive to work on ourselves comes from within and manifests as active participation in creating tangible differences in our lives and in the world around us. It is not enough to take something that was given to us and put it on a shelf to be forgotten or neglected. We must exert ourselves on all levels as we generate our own growth and evolution out of the Light we have received from Above.

Rosh Hashanah is essentially a day of judgment. On the deepest level, it calls forth within us the ability to self-judge, self-reflect and evaluate our life and actions, and to ask ourselves, 'Who am I, what is my purpose, and am I evolving toward that purpose?'

Yom Kippur then is best understood as the time when we come to encounter ourselves, who we really are, in pure honesty, without any add-ons, attachments or alterations. To do this, we strip away all of our externalities: we do not eat, drink, work, nor cushion our feet with leather shoes, nor anoint our skin with oils, nor engage in marital intimacy. We dress in pure white garments, stripping ourselves of all added 'colors'. On Yom Kippur we drop all our pretenses, our false self-images and self-definitions, in order to go very deeply into the question, 'Who am I *really*, without externalities, right here and right now?'

'If I subtract everything I surround myself with — my reliance on food, appearance, job, relationships, devices, entertainment, an ability to travel, etc. — what is my real identity? What do I really rely on?' Yom Kippur is a time to encounter yourself as you really are.

During the High Holidays, we need to be intensively asking ourselves, "Who am I? What is my purpose? And what do I need to let go of in order to connect to That which is much greater and loftier than me? How can I reach higher and touch Infinity?'

NUMERICAL VALUE OF THE NAME *Tishrei*: BUILDING HASHEM'S KINGSHIP

In Tishrei we reveal the meaning of a sentence that appears in our High Holy Day prayers, as well as in our daily prayers: *Hashem*

Melech, Hashem Malach, Hashem Yimloch l'Olam Va'ed / "Hashem reigns, Hashem has reigned, Hashem will reign for all eternity." These three short phrases come from *Tehilim* 10:16, *Tehilim* 93:1, and *Shemos* 15:18, respectively. The sources for uniting them into a single sentence are found in Zohar and Medrash.

Melech / king, in numerical value is 90 (Mem/40, Lamed/30, Chaf/20). The numerical value of the word *Tishrei* is 910 (Tav/400, Shin/300, Reish/200, Yud/10). The main letters of the word (without the Yud/10) have a numerical value of 900. This is ten times the value of the word *Melech* (90 x 10 = 900). *Hashem Melech* means Hashem is reigning over Creation now, in the present. Acknowledging that Hashem is King is part of the 'present moment' focus of Tishrei. Multiplying the word *Melech* by ten alludes to the fact that during the first ten days of Tishrei we have to confirm the Divine reign and build up Malchus in its ten dimensions: by raising up and revealing Hashem's Kingship throughout all the Ten Sefiros, and throughout all space and time, present, past and future.

As we begin the new year we also acknowledge that *Hashem Malach*, Hashem was ruling over our past. The words *Melech* / is king, and *Malach* / was king, have the same letters, and the same numerical value of 90. As we mentioned above, the full revelation of this value is 900. Yet, the fact that *Tishrei* is 900 plus 10 means that more is demanded of us than just confirming Hashem's reign over our past and present. Especially during the first ten days, we need to ensure that Hashem will be King over our future. We need to integrate the letter Yud (10) of the word *Tishrei*; when we add a Yud to *Melech* or to *Malach* it spells *Yimloch* / 'will' reign. In this way, Tishrei is about the present impregnating the future. The new year season gives birth to the fullness of the year to come.

Melech (90)	*Malach* (90)
Full expression of 90 is 900	
Tishrei (900 + Yud/10)	
Yimloch (90 + Yud/10)	

TISHREI = 19

It is worth mentioning a couple more relevant points relating to the numerical value of the word *Tishrei*. In *Mispar Katan /* small numeric value, Tishrei is 19.[*] Nineteen is the same value, in Mispar Katan, of the three special Mitzvos connected with the three holidays of Tishrei:

- *Shofar* = 19 [**]

- *Tashbisu*, or 'resting', which is the word the Torah uses to define Yom Kippur's rest (Vayikra, 23:32) = 19[***]

- *Sukkah* = 19 [****]

Tishrei is 910, and counting its vowels, is 960 (תִּשְׁרֵי — the Tav has the vowel Chirik, a dot under the letter, which is numerically equivalent to Yud (10). The Shin has the vowel Sh'va, two vertical dots, which is equivalent to two Yuds (20). The Reish has the vowel Tzeirei, which is two horizontal dots, also equivalent to two Yuds (20). In total there are then five Yuds, equalling 50. Thus,

---

[*] Tishrei: Tav (4), Shin (3), Reish (2), Yud (10) = 19
[**] Shofar: Shin (3), Vav (6), Pei (8), Reish (2) = 19
[***] Tashbisu: Tav (4), Shin (3), Beis (2), Tav (4), Vav (6) = 19
[****] Sukkah: Samach (6), Vav (6), Chaf (2), Hei (5) = 19

the consonants (910) plus the vowels (50) equal 960.) The 40 days from Elul through Yom Kippur also form the number 960: 40 times 24 hours equals 960 hours. As explored in *The Secret of Mikvah*, this forty day period is like a Mikvah within time. The amount of water that a Mikvah or purifying bath must contain is 40 Se'ah of water, an amount equal to 960 Lugin. By immersing intentionally in the 960 hours of this period we can attain a deep level of spiritual purity, which is a blessing as we begin the new year.

༁

SENSE

OUR CONVENTIONAL WORLD IDENTIFIES FIVE SENS-
ES, yet *Sefer Yetzirah* speaks of 12 *Chushin* / senses. In
addition to the more commonly understood definition
of a 'sense', the word *Chush* can also mean, 'a sensitive level of
perception, understanding, appreciation and skill' in relation to a
particular psycho-spiritual process or function. For example, a 'sense
of sleep' is a deep understanding and appreciation of sleep. This
understanding includes what sleep represents spiritually, as well
as the practical skills and techniques that make the experience of
sleep more peaceful and beneficial.

These twelve Chushim are also the twelve activities that the Torah describes the Creator performing in the perpetual process of maintaining the world (*Pirush haRavad, Sefer Yetzirah*). As we are created in the Divine image, we also possess the image of all twelve 'Divine Chushim', at least in potential.* Every month gives us the ability and strength to expand our vessels and potentials for a particular Chush, along with its corresponding Divine Attribute. When we align and refine our consciousness via these Chushim, we can harness the qualities of each month in a most profound and meaningful way.

According to Sefer Yetzirah, *the Chush* / sense connected with Tishrei is *Tashmish* / 'coition' or intimacy between spouses, and more generally, the sense of touch. The month of Tishrei, the headquarters of the year, imprints upon the entire year. One of the principal qualities that is imprinted is the 'sense' of intimacy with the Divine. The development of this Chush through the stages of this month moves from commitment, to our engagement, to wedding celebrations, and finally to intimacy and 'touch' with HaKadosh Baruch Hu, *Kaviyachol* / so-to-speak. This is an upward movement, from humanity below into the embrace and union with the Transcendent One, Above.

---

* Even if one is blind, for example, he always has the *potential* for sight — it is just that he is currently missing the physical vessels (capacity) for it (*Pirush haGra*, Hak'damah, Sefer Yetzirah). However, the sense of sight is included in the person's Divine image, as it were. Obviously, a physically blind person could have immense vessels for emotional, intellectual and spiritual sight.

In preparation for this awesome and deep sense of intimacy with Hashem we must first traverse the month of Elul, in which we cultivate a state of *Besulah* / spiritual 'virginity' (see the volume on the Month of Elul). The progression to intimacy begins with Rosh Hashanah and culminates with the last day of Sukkos and Shemini Atzeres / Simchas Torah. Rosh Hashanah is like a *Tenayim* / engagement ceremony, in which we, the bride, make a formal commitment to our Divine 'Fiancé'. On Yom Kippur we call out with abandon, from the depths of our heart and soul, 'I love You Hashem, I want to be with You, I want to feel Your presence at every moment!' Then we get married. During Sukkos we enter into a Chuppah with HaKadosh Baruch Hu and celebrate for seven days like the *Sheva B'rachos*, the seven days of the 'Seven Blessings', rejoicing with the groom and bride.

Our Chuppah with HaKadosh Baruch Hu is the Sukkah (Sukkah numerically is 91. The Name *Hashem*, the Transcendent One, represents the Groom. The Name *Ado-noi*, which is the way we pronounce *Hashem* today, represents the Feminine, the Bride. *Hashem* = 26 and *Ado-noi* = 65, totalling 91. The Yichud of the Bride (us) and the Groom (HaKadosh Baruch Hu). The Radbaz, *Metzudas David*, Mitzvah 117). The Halachic minimum enclosure for a Kosher Sukkah is two whole connected walls, plus a portion of a third wall. Says the AriZal, that this is symbolic of an embrace: ימינו תחבקני / "His right hand embraced me" (*Shir haShirim*, 8:3). That is, the two whole walls are like an arm and a chest, and the portion of a third wall is like a hand bent at the wrist, which surrounds us in a hug. This image embodies the quality of the Yom Tov of Sukkos (*Sha'ar haKavanos*, Derushei Chag haSukos, Derush 4), a time when we feel embraced and protected by HaKadosh Baruch Hu (The Targum, *ad loc.*, teaches that "His right hand embraced me" refers to the

Mitzvah of Mezuzah that is placed on the right side of the doorpost, and protects the home from all negative influences).

When you are embraced in a small, partial hug you are surrounded by a chest, an arm extending around your side, and a hand on your back. A complete hug wraps fully around you, like a full four-walled Sukkah. Hence, many pious individuals desire to build their Sukkos fully surrounded, going beyond the minimum requirement of Halacha / Torah Law.

When we build the Sukkah, we do so according to the instructions of the Torah and Chazal, symbolizing our resolve, commitment and desire to live a G-dly life, a life infused with meaning and purpose, in intimacy with HaKadosh Baruch Hu. Having prepared the vessel in this way, then שם שמים / the Name of Hashem comes upon the Sukkah (*Sukkah*, 9a). We create the physical space of the Sukkah and then Hashem's Presence rests upon the Sukkah and we become enveloped within the Divine embrace.

Genuine encounters demand presence and focus, and certainly if they are as deep as intimacy with a spouse. They require being fully in the present, without your mind wandering to other people, to other subjects, or to an unrelated past or future. Being in a state of presence means to be in the eternal moment that both transcends and encompasses all time, past, present and future. The spiritual intimacy of Sukkos similarly transcends and includes all of time. We rest in the embrace, the love our Beloved, affectionately remembering Rosh Hashanah and Yom Kippur, our commitment, and the days leading up to our wedding. We are present with each other as we celebrate and excitedly imagine and dream of our possible future together. (סוכה / Sukkah, being under the open sky under the stars, is connected to the word סכה / *Socheh* / deeper seeing, seeing with *Ruach HaKodesh* / holy intuition, as it were: Rabbeinu Bachya, *Kad Kemach*, Sukkah. למה נקרא שמה יסכה? שסכתה ברוח הקודש: *Megilah*, 14b. See also Maharal, *Gevuros Hashem*, 46. Sukkos in general is a time for Ruach haKodesh: Yerushalmi, *Sukkah*, 5:1). By going out into the Sukkah, we declare to our Beloved: "This year I am ready to go wherever You want me to go — even to a tent out in the cold — so long as I will be with You."

Finally, on Shemini Atzeres, the Divine *Chibuk* / embrace of Sukkos culminates in deep *Zivug* / intimacy, and *Yichud* / unity between Klal Yisrael and HaKadosh Baruch Hu. Our sages tell us, both in *Tikkunei Zohar* and the Gemara, that physical intimacy should be performed with no separation or intervening *Levushim* or 'garments'. It should be Etzem to Etzem, essence to essence, flesh to flesh.* In an essence-to-essence encounter there should not, nor could there really be, any form of intermediary or intervening *Levushim* / garments. When this deepest form of 'touch', essence to essence, is performed "in the right time, with the correct intention" it can be the holiest of acts (*Igeres Kodesh*, attributed to the Rambam, Chap. 2. Instead of it being merely a *Cherpah* / disgrace, in the language of other Rishonim. Rambam, *Moreh Nevuchim*, 3:8. *Sefer haChinuch*, Mitzvah 117). And for this action to be full unity, there needs to be full touch, without any intermediaries.

---

* *Tikkunei Zohar*, Tikkun 58. שארה זו קרוב בשר שלא ינהג בה מנהג פרסיים שמשמשין מטותיהן בלבושיהן...האומר אי אפשי אלא אני בבגדי והיא בבגדה יוציא ונותן כתובה / *She'era* refers to closeness of flesh, which teaches that he should not treat her in the manner of Persians, who have conjugal relations in their clothes… One who says, 'I do not want to be intimate with my wife, unless I am in my clothes and she is in her clothes,' must divorce his wife and give her the payment for her marriage contract": *Kesuvos*, 48a. ואף על פי שעושה כן לצניעות / "even if he wants to do so for the purpose of modesty": *Shita Mekubetzes*, as loc. *Ritvah*, ad loc. See also, *Beis Yoseph*, Even haEzer, 76:21:1

On Sukkos, we enter with our entire body into the Sukkah, with no intermediary. Every Mitzvah is an opportunity to connect with HaKadosh Baruch Hu on a revealed level. Every Mitzvah opens us up to live, consciously and intentionally, in 'Divine space'. Every Mitzvah is an invitation to intimacy with the Giver of the Mitzvah. Yet a Sukkah is unique in that we actually enter into the Mitzvah, and do so without any 'item' in hand, without any 'intermediary' Levushim or *Kelim* / vessels. (In the language of Chazal, Kelim can mean Levushim).

All Mitzvos are action-based, whether they involve physical actions or mental or verbal actions. All Mitzvos of physical action have a particular physical item through which the Mitzvah is performed. For example, on Rosh Hashanah we hold a Shofar in our hand and blow it, and on Pesach we eat Matzah. In this way, a physical object allows us to connect to the Giver of Mitzvos, the Source of Life, and participate in revealing the *Ohr* / Light that is shining during these Holy Days. The Mitzvah of Sukkah is utterly unique. It too demands an action, the building of a certain structure, yet we do not hold the Mitzvah with our hands nor blow it or eat it with our mouth. Rather, we enter it fully and 'live' there. This is in contrast to the Mitzvah of Mikvah. We also enter fully inside that Mitzvah, but when we are underwater we cease breathing and 'living'.

With the Sukkah, there is no particular 'item' or 'object' which would be associated with a particular part of our body. Rather, our whole self, the essence of self, connects with the essence of the Mitzvah (Perhaps the Mitzvah of living in Eretz Yisrael is also a full-body-immersion Mitzvah).

When we enter completely into the Mitzvah, into the embrace of the Sukkah with no separation, we are present, intimately so, without any need for a Levush or Kli. We do not need an inter-mediating item, since our entire body enters the Sukkah. We are surrounded and subsumed within the Mitzvah, encompassed by Hashem's embrace. We are utterly and fully unified with Hashem in a direct encounter, essence-to-Essence.

Parenthetically, there is a custom of dancing on Sukkos, since *Chag* / festival also means 'dance', as the Netziv writes (*HaAmek Davar*, Devarim, 16:15. See also Tosefos Yom Tov, *Rosh Hashanah*, 1:2). We dance during the days of Simchas Beis haShoeivah and then on Simchas Torah. Dancing is very embodied; it is not by nature ethereal, cerebral or detached from the body. Dancing is touch; whether stamping with your feet on the ground, as is the custom for many, or lightly gliding, this type of activity is connected to the sense of this month, the sense of touch.

THE SENSE OF TOUCH: ESSENCE-TO-ESSENCE

To summarize, in all true intimacy, there needs to be a) involve-ment with the entire body, both literally and metaphorically, and b) direct contact, without Levushim.

While this is true of full human intimacy, it is also true to some extent, regarding the sense of touch itself, the sense of this month. Touch is connected to the entire body, and it is by definition a direct experience. The tactile sense is the only one of the five senses that is felt throughout the entire body; the other senses are located more exclusively in the head, as in eyes, ears, nose, or mouth (for this reason, among others, the hand Tefillin, connected to touch, has one box, whereas the head Tefillin, connected to the other four senses within the head, has four boxes: Rosh, *Shemos*, 13:16. *Prisha*, Orach Chayim, 32:34:1).

Besides being present throughout the body wherever there is skin, the experience of touch is 'direct'; there is unmitigated contact between subject and object. This is unlike seeing, hearing or smelling, which involve the indirect processing of waves, vibrations or projections. To see, the eye detects images of visible light on the photoreceptors of the retina of the eye and that generates electrical nerve impulses in the brain. To hear, vibrations are detected by the ear and transduced into nerve impulses that are perceived by the brain. To smell, scent is released from the object and detected by the olfactory receptor neurons in the nose. Yet, touch, relative to the other senses, is immediate, without a process of translation.

The Rambam writes that we do not find anywhere in the Torah that Hashem 'touches' (nor 'tastes' which is a sense received through touch), although we do find expressions of Hashem 'hearing', 'seeing' and taking pleasure in 'smell'. The reason, writes the Rambam, is that touch is direct; it only occurs in close contact. Touch and taste only register when in direct contact with the object, whereas sight, hearing, and smell can register even distant objects — and Hashem 'distantly' Transcends Creation (*Moreh Nevuchim*, 1:47).

Touch is also considered the most physical of the senses. In the language of the Maharal, כי כל כוח גשמי היא פועל במישוש / "for all physicality functions through the world of touch" (*Chidushei Agados*, Avodah Zarah, 25a). By definition, a physical body 'touches' a physical object. Hashem, the Transcendent One, is not in any sense corporeal or physical in nature (Rambam, *Mishnah Sanhedrin*, 10:1).

Everything has both an עצם / *Etzem* / essence, which is the entirety of the thing itself, and a dimension of גילוי / *Gilui* / revealing or projection. All senses except touch are perceived through the Gilui of the object, meaning its appearance or light wave, its sound or vibration, or its projected airborne particles or scent. Touch is contact with the Etzem of the object itself. We feel the actual object, not merely its wave, vibration or scent. Thus, touch seems to be a 'lower' sense, not located in the head, the seat of 'intelligence'. Rather it seems to be dispersed throughout the entire body, and it is the most 'physical' sense. Yet, since touch is direct, in a way it is much deeper than the other senses. It is Etzem-to-Etzem.

In general, the five senses correspond to the five inner worlds (Keser / Adam Kadmon, Atzilus, Beriyah, Yetzirah, and Asiyah) and the five dimensions of the Name of Hashem (the four letters plus the *Kotz* / point atop the Yud). Physical touch corresponds to the material world of Asiyah, and progressing upwards and inwards is the next, more refined, ethereal sense of taste, then sight, which can be observed from a distance and is not tactile. Then comes hearing, which is more ethereal and less tangible than sight, and finally smell.

SENSE	WORLD	LETTER OR 'DIMENSION' OF THE DIVINE NAME
Smell	Keser / Adam Kadmon	Kotz shel Yud
Hearing	Atzilus	Yud
Sight	Beriyah	Upper Hei
Taste	Yetzirah	Vav
Touch	Asiyah	Lower Hei

Yet, from another perspective, the 'lowest' most physical of the senses, the sense of touch, is paradoxically connected to the highest source. The great Mekubal, Rav Yoseph Tzayach or Taitazak (a teacher of Rav Shlomo Alkabetz and Rav Yoseph Caro) writes that the sense of touch is connected to the innermost level of Keser, the highest and deepest realm of existence (*Even haShoham*, Chap. 8). This is because touch is the sense of *Etzem* / Essence, so-to-speak.

SENSE	WORLD	LETTER OF DIVINE NAME
Touch Direct, Complete Contact	Keser / Adam Kadmon / Etzem and Entirety of All Worlds	Kotz shel Yud / Etzem and Entirety of the Name

Today, in the world of exile and *Pirud* / separation, we live in a world of Hashem's גילוים / *Giluyim* / revelations, or lack thereof. At times we experience Hashem's revealed expression of *Chesed* / Divine Compassion and kindness, and at times we experience Hashem's revelation as *Din* / Divine judgment and concealment. Chesed and Din are both within the realm of גילוים / revealed expressions of Hashem; neither of them are the עצם / *Etzem* / Essence of Hashem, as it were. There will come a time, however, when Hashem's Etzem will become 'revealed' within the essence of this world. Then we will be able to 'touch' Hashem; we will be able to experience our essence in Unity with the Essence of HaKadosh Baruch Hu, *Kaviyachol* / so-to-speak.

Actually, this type of Etzem-to-Etzem relationship with HaKadosh Baruch Hu and with all of Creation is something we experienced in the beginning of time, in Gan Eden, as "the beginning and end are wedged together." The beginning and end are both of Etzem, whereas all the movement in between pertains to the world of *Giluyim* / revelation.

In the world of *Pirud* / separation, the world of Giluyim, every pleasure we experience is through a particular *Giluy* / expression or aspect of ourselves, as opposed to the entirety of ourselves. In addition, the object that we are having pleasure from is also just revealing an aspect of the object, not its essence or entirety.

In our world today, every pleasure that we receive comes to us through two constricting and limiting Giluyim:

1) There is a Giluy of the object of pleasure, a thing or person which is 'giving' the pleasure, and 2) there is a Giluy, a specific part of the body that is 'receiving' the pleasure (*Sefer haDe'ah* II, Derush 4, 11:4). Take for example, the pleasure of eating a fruit. We may eat the 'entire' fruit, but really it is only the flavor and texture that 'give' us pleasure, and not other aspects of the fruit. In other words, only the גילוים of taste and texture within the fruit are revealed to us and stimulate pleasure. Also, it is only our Giluyim, our taste buds within our mouth, that 'receive' the pleasure, and we are not feeling the pleasure in other parts of the body.

When Adam and Chavah ate from the Tree of Knowledge, the paradigm of opposites and separation, they became perceptually separated from Gan Eden and the Tree of Life. Ever since then, humanity in general experiences life from a place of Giluyim. Yet, there will come a time (which is the Essence and depth of all time, including that of the present time) when Etzem will become perceptually 'revealed'. Then we will no longer experience a physical, existential and spiritual exile, rather we will experience Hashem's Presence and all of Hashem's Creation without Giluyim, pure essence to Essence. There will no longer be any separation, thus no longer any *Levushim* / garments or intermediaries between us and life, between subject and object, or between ourselves and the Source of Life. Then the entirety of a piece of fruit will 'touch' the essence and entirety of the self. And our entire self will take pleasure not only from the entirety of the fruit, but also the Creator of the fruit.

ROSH HASHANAH, YOM KIPPUR & SUKKOS, AS CONNECTED TO ETZEM

As explained, Sukkos and the Sukkah itself are connected to Etzem, as they are directly in contact with the Mitzvah. Sitting in a Sukkah is a direct, full-body revelation, as it were, of the Etzem of the *Ohr* / light of Sukkos.

Rosh Hashanah is a time of Divine judgment, a time when the Creator of All Life conceptually asks us to give 'reasons' why we exist and why we should exist, as will be explored later in this text, and in *Murmurings of Majesty: the Mysteries of Shofar & Rosh*

Hashanah. In this way, Rosh Hashanah too is an 'existential' day of Etzem.

Yom Kippur is all about Etzem, as well. Regarding the day of Yom Kippur, the Torah says, וכל־מלאכה לא תעשו בעצם היום הזה כי יום כפרים הוא / "You shall do no work throughout the essence of this day, for it is a Day of Atonement." The Torah here uses the unusual phrase *Etzem* regarding a Yom Tov (*Etzem* is also used for Shavuos), and this, as the Ramban explains (*Vayikra*, 23:28), is the reason for Chazal saying עיצומו של יום הכפורים מכפר לשבים / "The essence of the day brings atonement, for those who do Teshuvah" (Rambam, *Hilchos Teshuvah*, 1:3. In other words, all opinions agree that עיצומו של יום הכפורים מכפר the argument is whether this is with or without Teshuvah: Rebbe Yehudah and the *Chachamim* / sages, *Shavuos*, 13a. *Yuma*, 85b).

Rosh Hashanah, Yom Kippur and Sukkos will be explored in greater detail and within the context of the month of Tishrei further on.

☾

♈

SIGN

E ACH MONTH CONTAINS THE ZODIAC INFLUENCE OF A particular constellation, called a *Mazal*. A constellation is a perceivably patterned grouping of visible stars. Today, we count 88 constellations in the night sky. Out of all of these, one constellation is predominantly visible on the horizon at the beginning of each month.

Each constellation refracts the light of the cosmos differently, alternately reflecting times that are more conducive to war, and times that are more conducive for peace to flourish, for example (*Yalkut Reuveini*, Bereishis, Os 56). The Zohar teaches that each sign can manifest positively or negatively (*Zohar* 3, 282a). In other words, the constellations can have either a productive or a destructive influence in one's life. It is not because the created cluster of stars actually have any real influence, rather, the sky's formation is an indication and external expression of how Hashem is, *Kaviyachol* / so-to-speak, interacting with Creation at this moment.

It is also important to keep in mind that whether our proclivities seem to be innate or celestially influenced, we always possess the free choice to respond to the situations that arise in our life. We can choose how to reflect back what has been projected onto us, even from the stars. For example, a person born under the influence of Mars, "the Red Planet", may have a tendency to be connected in some way to 'blood', and that is part of their Tikkun. Nevertheless, he also has the ability to employ this tendency for good or ill; he could choose to be a violent criminal or a life-saving surgeon.

Due to the prevailing popular belief that the stars exert a kind of fatalistic influence upon world history and human development, we need to repeatedly emphasize that anyone can rise above such influences altogether and be unaffected by them. Despite all the forces and influences in our life — physical and psychological conditions, upbringing, education, environment, financial status, etc. — we always have the freedom to choose. We have the choice to live as either the *effect* of our conditions (as passive receivers of what life serves us), or as the *cause* of what comes next, as proactive co-creators of our lives. When we begin to live more proactively, the influences of our birth constellation and the *Mazal* of each month function less as positive or negative *influences* and more as *tools* that can help us climb ever higher into our freedom of being.

Moznayim / Libra, represented by the image of scales, is the astrological sign of this month. Tishrei stands in between the heat of the summer and the cold of the winter, between the dry and wet season, and as such, Tishrei is the month of scales or 'balance' (*Pirush haRavad*, Sefer Yetzirah).

Experientially and inwardly, the balancing of scales is related to Rosh Hashanah and Yom Kippur, when our past actions are 'weighed', hopefully to reveal how virtuous we were (See Ran, *Rosh Hashanah,* 16a). If not, we are given the opportunity, through Teshuvah, prayer, and acts of charity, to nullify all *Din* / judgment or negative effects coming from our past actions and start a new, fresh year. Teshuvah is when we weigh our lives and ascertain that our priorities are, if needed, rebalanced and recalibrated. Regarding the words in *Tehilim* (62:10) במאזנים לעלות / "elevated on the scale", the Medrash says, "All vanities which Israel does all the days of the year are elevated (i.e., vanish) on the scales. The Holy One, blessed be He, pardons them in the constellation *Moznayim* / Libra, Scales (*Tanchuma,* Shelach, 13:1).

As we mentioned previously, the letter of the month, Lamed, alludes to *Limud* / learning. People born in Tishrei have an inclination toward intellectual pursuit, and a strong desire to learn and understand everything. With such a desire, Libras tend to have equal interest in many areas of life, and often experience difficulties with decision-making. Tishrei gives all of us an opportunity for Tikkun by calling us to weigh everything in our life, make firm decisions, and rebalance our priorities.

TRIBE

EVERY MONTH OF THE YEAR IS CONNECTED WITH ONE OF the Twelve Tribes of Israel, named after one of the sons of Yaakov (*Sefer Yetzirah*. Medrash, *Osyos Rebbe Akiva*, Dalet).

The tribe of this month is Ephrayim. Yoseph, the son of Yaakov, is subdivided into two tribes, Ephrayim and Menasheh (Tishrei is the seventh month of the year and Yoseph is the seventh child of Yaakov: Maharal, *Chidushei Agados*, Rosh Hashanah 11a). The root of the word *Ephrayim* means 'fruitful'. When he was born, Yoseph gave him the name Ephrayim, saying, "…for Hashem has caused me to be fruitful in the land of my affliction"(*Bereishis*, 41:52). Yoseph had been sold into slavery and was living in exile in Egypt, away from his beloved father, when he declared that even in a place of affliction and hardship Hashem had caused him to be fruitful and prosperous, and specifically fruitful with the blessing of healthy children.

The letter of the month is Lamed. As above, 'Lamed' alludes to *Limud* / learning and *Lameid* / teaching others. Our sages tell us that someone who teaches Torah to another זוכה לברכות כיוסף / merits to receive blessings as did Yoseph (*Sanhedrin*, 92a). Sharing Torah teachings opens us to receive blessings of fruitfulness and children, even amid apparent hardship.

אפרים / Ephrayim comes from the same root word that the Torah uses in commanding and empowering Adam and Chavah to have children: פרו /"Be fruitful" and multiply (*Bereishis*, 1:28). This is the first and fundamental Mitzvah that Adam and Chavah and all future generations received. The Mitzvah to procreate is achieved through physical intimacy and touch — the sense of this month.

On Rosh Hashanah, the first day of Tishrei, we say in our prayers, *HaYom Haras Olam* / "Today the world becomes pregnant" (the pregnancy is in Tishrei, the birth is in Nisan: *Pri Eitz Chayim*, Sha'ar haShofar, 5). The world is pregnant with new possibilities, new life, new potential that can be actualized in the coming year. During this month of blessings of being fruitful, we 'conceive' a fruitful new year. The blessings are drawn down during Rosh Hashanah and in Tishrei and then 'birthed' or unpacked and articulated throughout the coming year.

Yoseph had two older boys, Menasheh and Ephrayim. He calls his oldest son Menasheh, because כי-נשני אלקים את-כל-עמלי / "G-d has made me forget my hardship completely" (*Bereishis*, 41:51). The second son he calls Ephrayim because "Hashem has caused me to be fruitful in the land of my affliction." There is a clear distinction here between the names of these two children. The oldest son is about the past; thanking Hashem for allowing him to forget his past and his hardships up until this point. The younger son is named for the blessings Hashem has given him now, in the present. The first is about "forgetting" or letting go of the past, and the second is about building a future, "being fruitful" despite being in a land of affliction.

Elul is the final month of the past year, in which we dealt with and undertook Teshuvah for our past. That Teshuvah was more focused on regret and remorse for mistakes. Tishrei is a new beginning. We move away from the whole issue of our past. Even our Teshuvah is now more focused on *Kabbalah* / acceptance of new patterns of behavior, intending a new beginning and a new year. Despite having lived in a 'land of affliction', of mistakes and misalignments, we are now focussed fully on living with a deep resolve for a brighter, holier, more mindful and fruitful future.

This, the *Koach* / power of Ephrayim, and the blessing that Yoseph received, we also receive. Our fruitfulness is greatly increased when we extend ourselves to teach another person, especially during this month.

In Tishrei we actively pursue positivity, and do not merely turn away from our past negativity. Our primary mandate in Tishrei, and in the new year, is to dwell in the present and move forward, creating a brighter present and future. We focus on prospering and being fruitful in the present in a way that blesses our future.

Just as Menasheh is about the past and Ephrayim is about the future, Klal Yisrael learns from its past, but moves toward its future. We live with hope, with dreams, with anticipation and yearning, for our future fruition in an era of redemption. Klal Yisrael, as a whole, embodies and expresses these qualities of Ephrayim so much that the name of the entire People, not only the descendants of his tribe, is called 'Ephrayim'. In the book of Yirmiyahu the Prophet, Hashem says of Klal Yisrael, "Is Ephrayim not My dear son, the child in whom I delight? …My heart yearns for him; I have great compassion for him" (*Yirmiyahu*, 31:20). We recall our past but live in the present, with our eyes on the future; always dreaming and imagining a better world, and ultimately hoping for the revealing of Moshiach, speedly in our days.

BODY PART

ACH MONTH IS CONNECTED WITH THE QUALITIES OF a particular body part. This interinclusion of the body within time empowers us to focus on and refine the spiritual properties and miraculous functionings of our physical body, as the spiral of the yearly cycle continues to turn on its Divine axis. The body part associated with Tishrei is the *Marah* / gallbladder. This organ sits just beneath the liver and stores bile, a bitter dark green to yellowish-brown fluid produced by the liver that aids digestion. When food that contains fat enters the digestive tract, the gallbladder releases bile to help break it down.

Marah literally means 'bitter', referring to bile or guile. Many ancient physicians, and as codified by some of the Rishonim (for example, Rabbi Meir Aldavie, *Shevilei Emunah*, Nasiv 4), speak of the four humors of the body: blood, phlegm, yellow bile, and black bile, and that the health of the body depends on having a perfect equilibrium (alluding to Libra, the Mazal of the month) between these four humors. Not only do they influence our physical health, but also our emotions. We need to take care of our physical health to ensure that our emotional health is in balance, as often an imbalance in the body will affect one's emotional state. For example, it's possible a person feels depressed or sad when really they are simply physically tired and their minds are merely telling them a self-defeating story. This can also happen visa versa. Although it can be a little more difficult, when we take excellent care of our emotional and mental state and live with balance, it has a powerful effect on the physical health of our body.

An excess of *Marah Shechorah* / black bile causes melancholy and lethargic behavior. In fact, the English word 'melancholy' comes from the Greek term for black bile. A properly elevated level of *Marah L'veinah* / white bile causes more spirited and joyful behavior and temperament.

The *Marah* / gallbladder is specifically associated with yellow or green bile, connected with phlegm. *Marah Yerukah* / green or yellow bile is connected with cravings and obsessive behavior. An excess of Marah Yerukah can result in impulsive, rash, tempered, or domineering behavior. We need to ensure, throughout the entire year, that our behaviors are in balance. Actively engaging in the practices of Tishrei, the month of *Moznayim* / Libra / Scales of Judgment, gives us more *Koach* / power to achieve that perfect balance.

It is worth pointing out that *Sefer Yetzirah* teaches that gall-bladder and coition are related. This is a reminder that one should ensure a 'Libra' or balanced approach regarding one's intimate relationships, and clearly avoid any impulsive, domineering or unwholesome behaviors. This too is part of the Tikkun of Tishrei.

℞

ELEMENT

THERE ARE FOUR PRIMARY ELEMENTS OR BUILDING BLOCKS of Creation: fire, air, water and earth. Each month is associated with one of these four elements. However, it is important to note that while manifesting physically, these elements are also meant to be understood in a metaphysical sense as well, as they represent numerous spiritual properties, qualities, and correspondences.

Tishrei is the element of Wind. Wind and air represent the gift of flexibility, openness, the ability not to be stuck in preconceived or imbalanced ideas or behaviors. The previous month with the element of wind was Sivan, when we collectively and individually received the Torah, the first set of the *Luchos* / Tablets. But, sadly, we were not emotionally, mentally or spiritually ready and equipped to stabilize ourselves within the radical teachings of the Torah, of Monotheism, of the Oneness of Hashem. Due to our own spiritual imbalances and brokenness, the first Luchos were broken and fragmented. Because we were still inwardly fragmented and not ready for true unity and wholeness to be revealed, we worshiped a fragment, a brokenness, a mere part of the Whole. It was thus fitting that the Luchos we received were broken as a result. In the month of Tishrei, and specifically on the day of Yom Kippur, the Day of Atonement, we were forgiven and restored to wholeness, balance and inner stability. On each Yom Kippur we are forgiven in the same way: the old is erased and elevated, and the new beginning ensues. It is a day of wholeness and at-one-ment, that we achieve out of our place of brokenness. It is a deep healing that occurs after the fragmentation of sin. It is a day when we rise up from the ashes, reach up and touch our pure, unified essence.

On Yom Kippur we received — and every year we receive again — the second set of Luchos, the Luchos that are never broken, that are always whole. On a deeper level, the Second Luchos reveal a wholeness that is within the brokenness, whole despite the brokenness we may experience in life. This is the idea of 'being fruitful and multiplying' within a place of hardship.

☾

TORAH PORTIONS

O VER THE COURSE OF A MONTH, 4-5 WEEKLY TORAH portions are read by the community. These individual portions can be combined and viewed as a single unit based on the particular month in which they are most commonly read. Indeed, one finds, when viewing the Torah Portions through this calendrical lens, that an astounding array of thematic elements consistent with the spiritual energy of the month is revealed.

In Tishrei we mostly read the Torah portions that are chosen for, and to reflect, the month's Holy Days. These chapters and passages from the Torah speak of birth, renewal, starting over, a sense of purpose, forgiveness and joy. On Simchas Torah we complete the cycle of portions from the previous year, wrap up the scroll, and then begin reading the first portion of *Bereishis*, Genesis — the portion of a new Creation and new beginnings. All these readings are clearly connected to this month of Tishrei, a time of new beginnings, of starting over again, of being unburdened by the past and feeling inner joy.

SEASON OF THE YEAR

THE SEASONAL QUALITIES OF EACH MONTH ARE intricately related with the spiritual qualities of that month. When daylight lasts for either longer or shorter times, different kinds of spiritual light are being revealed on a subtle level. The physical experiences of spring are external expressions of an internal reality that emanates during that time, such as the vital pulse of new life and growth. All dark, cold months reflect an energy of corresponding spiritual 'coldness', stimulating us to seek warmth. People tend to keep to themselves when winter begins and are more outgoing when summer starts. All of these psychophysical weather patterns reflect deeper spiritual truths, as the mind-body complex is a reflection of the metaphysical qualities of the soul and spiritual realm.

Tishrei falls during the Gregorian months of September and October, around the Autumnal Equinox, a time when the sun rises directly in the east and sets directly in the west, when the day and night are of equal length. It is also when the heat of the summer is over, yet the rainy season of the fall has not yet fully begun. It is neither too hot nor too cold. In this way, the season itself alludes to the 'balance' of Moznayim, and it is a time to recalibrate and rebalance our actions and mindset.

During the Tishrei season, as the summer has come to a close, vacations are over and students are returning to school. Psychologically and inwardly speaking, the fresh state of mind that can result is an opportunity to begin new projects or new life paths. This state parallels the newness experienced in Nisan, the first month of the spring. Nisan, however, is the beginning of the warm season, accompanied by new growth and spontaneous, miraculous blessings from Above, whereas Tishrei is a time for 'natural' beginnings, and lifting oneself up by actively choosing. A time of Teshuvah, a time of judgment and self-judgment, and a time of atonement. Tishrei is a posture from 'below to above'; we are desiring to reach inwards and upwards, to learn more, to grow in knowledge, and to 'multiply' or prosper physically, emotionally, mentally and spiritually.

The Torah calls the month of Tishrei "the Seventh Month". The construct of seven suggests the fullness of the natural cycle of time; there are seven days of the week and the seven years of a Shemitah work-rest cycle, when for six years the land is cultivated and on the seventh it lays fallow. Incidentally, the month of the Gregorian calendar that most often coincides with Tishrei is September, which comes from the Latin word *Septem* meaning seven. Tishrei is the season of 'seven', the natural world, and just like Shabbos elevates the six days of the natural work-week, and Shemitah elevates the six years, the seventh month, elevates the months.

Shabbos and Shemita complete their preceding time periods, and they also serve as an inspiration and harbinger for the quality of the coming time periods. Similarly, Tishrei comes after the completion of the six months of spring and summer, and begins the six months of autumn and winter; it completes the past and inspires the future. Tishrei is like the Shabbos, the *Mekor haBerachos* / source of blessings, of the yearly cycle.

The intensive spiritual work of Tishrei is analogous to the agrarian harvest of this season. With effort, we gather unto ourselves the traits and habits that will nourish us during the coming year, and we cast away those that are spoiled or harmful. Having dealt with these lower issues and having re-balanced our lives, we can now ascend to higher spiritual states. For this reason, the theme of the month is אתערותא דלתתא / *Isarusa d'le Tata* / 'awakening from below' and gathering our strength in order to elevate the year ahead.

We are on the ladder of life, and no matter which rung we are on, even if we are very low, if we are facing upwards, and if upwards is our goal and ambition, then we are set to climb. Tishrei orients us upward and gives us the joyful strength to move higher.

ॐ

THE HOLIDAYS
OF THE MONTH

OR EVERYTHING THERE IS AN APPOINTED TIME" (*Koheles*, 3:1). In other words, everything happens according to Divine timing (Rebbe Rayatz, *Sefer haMa'amarim*, Tav-Shin-Aleph, p. 59). When we left Egypt, it was the appointed time for such liberation. Indeed, Nisan is the perfect month for the Exodus and Redemption. King David in the book of Psalms says, "Hashem מוציא אסירים בכושרות / sets free the imprisoned" (*Tehilim*, 68:7). The word כושרות is related to the word כשר / Kosher, meaning, Hashem took us out of prison, from Egypt, in a Kosher, appropriate month. Hashem took us out, says Rabbi Akiva (*Medrash Rabbah*, Bamidbar, 3:6), in a month that is perfect to be taken out, perfect for travelling in the desert, a month that is not too hot nor too cold (see also Rashi, ad loc. *Mechilta deRabbi Yishmael*, Bo, 16, on *Tehillim*, 68:7. Rashi, *Sotah*, 2a).

This means not only that Pesach occurred in the historically appropriate time, but also at the right time of year — the season best suited for this expression of Redemption. This is the same principle behind every Yom Tov: the narrative and observance of each celebration or fast reflects and refracts the light of the natural world through a spiritual lens.

Furthermore, in the months that contain a *Yom Tov* / holiday, that Yom Tov embodies and encapsulates the quality of the entire month in condensed form. In a month that does not have a major holiday, that absence is also an expression of the unique quality of the month.

Tishrei does not only have one Yom Tov, rather it is a month 'saturated' with holidays. It is the seventh month, seven is שבע / *Sheva* in Hebrew. שבע is related to the word

שבוע / satisfied, satiated. The seventh month of the year is satiated with holiness, full of Yom Tovs, from Rosh Hashanah, to Yom Kippur, Sukkos and Simchas Torah. The following are the most simple descriptions of these Yom Tovs.

ROSH HASHANAH

Rosh Hashanah is the day of judgment and a time to coronate HaKadosh Baruch Hu as the King of the Universe. The entire quality of the year, whether we are materially prosperous or not, whether our year will be filled with eternity, depth and true life or not, is contingent on Rosh Hashanah. All potential spiritual blessings of the year are downloaded on the first day of Rosh Hashanah, and all potential material blessings are downloaded on the second day. Rosh Hashanah literally means the 'Head of the Year'. Just as the head is the headquarters of the entire body's vitality and sensory consciousness that is then distributed throughout the entire body, so too, Rosh Hashanah is the headquarters through which all vitality and consciousness must pass as it is distributed throughout the entire year. Our year depends on our Rosh Hashanah.

YOM KIPPUR

While Rosh Hashanah is primarily a day of judgment, Yom Kippur is the meta-root of all Teshuvah and forgiveness. The first ten days of Tishrei are called the 'Ten Days of Teshuvah'. It is a time, as our sages say (*Rosh Hashanah*, 18a), when the verse "Seek Hashem when He may be found; call on Him when He is near" (*Yeshayahu*, 55:6), is most applicable. It is a time when "the Source of Light is drawn to its sparks" (Mitteler Rebbe, *Derech Chaim*, p 13d). This is true for all ten days. However, the tenth day, Yom Kippur, (which is the Malchus and the Keser of the ten days) is the peak of this sense of nearness.

Yom Kippur is called *Achas b'Shanah*, the 'singularity of the year', or the oneness at the center-point of the flow of time. The word שנה / *Shanah* / year is etymologically related to the word שינוי / *Shinui* / change. The rhythmic flow of the year, from evening to morning, from fall to winter, from spring to summer, is an expression of the multiplicity and constant changing nature of Creation. The seasons are in a perpetual state of flux, and so are we; we have ups and downs, better days and worse, days when we live (in a revealed way) connected to Hashem Echad, and days when we are off the mark, and descend into a world of (apparent) separation. There are days when we live as the 'cause' of life, and days when we live as the effect of life. And yet, at the core of this vast field of movement of time and consciousness stands the immoveable, still, unaffected and unchanging dimension of *Achas* / oneness. This is the stainless purity of Yom Kippur, which is one with *Yechidah* / the oneness within our deepest selves.

In this light we can see that Yom Kippur is also a beginning, a foundation, a new place to emerge. On this day we can start all over again, with a clean slate, in a vast space of forgiveness and Teshuvah. Yom Kippur is a space where we are still and not affected by life's turbulence; it is a day of perfect balance. Appropriately, the only time that the written Torah employs the phrase *Rosh Hashanah* is in reference to Yom Kippur (*Yechezkel*, 40:1). Indeed, Yom Kippur is considered a 'new year' with regard to certain Torah laws, such as setting slaves free. On Yom Kippur of the Jubilee Year, slaves could go free and return to their proper homes. Thus, Yom Kippur allows us to begin afresh, and return to our true 'home' within.

SUKKOS

Sukkos also has an element of the ending of the previous year, and the beginning of the new year. The Torah calls Sukkos a Yom Tov that comes בצאת השנה / "as the year ends" (*Shemos*, 23:16). Similarly, with regards to *Hakhel* (the Mitzvah of Grand Assembly, in the eighth year, following the Shemitah year) the Torah calls the Yom Tov of Sukkos מקץ שבע שנים / the *Keitz* / end of the (previous) seven years (*Devarim*, 31:10). Clearly, the Torah views the entire holiday season, from Rosh Hashanah through Sukkos, as the end of the previous year and the beginning of the new year.

More pertinently, the verse says תקעו בחודש שופר בכסה ליום חגנו / "Blow the horn on the new moon, on the full moon for our feast day" (*Tehilim*, 81:4). This verse can also be read in this way: 'The effects of blowing the horn on the new moon, when the moon is concealed (בכסה), become revealed on יום חגנו / the Day of our Festivity — the Yom Tov of Sukkos' (*Likutei Torah*, Rosh Hashanah, 54d. *Siddur Im Dach*, 235b). Rosh Hashanah occurs on the first day of the month, when the moon is concealed* and hidden from the

---

* The "concealed moon" also alludes to the fact that Tishrei is the only month of the year that we do not bless the moon beforehand; we do not hold the Torah on the preceding Shabbos and announce the date of the new moon of Rosh Chodesh Tishrei and bless the upcoming month. There are various reasons for this:

  1) Since Rosh Chodesh Tishrei is also Rosh Hashanah, there is no need to announce before when Rosh Chodesh will be: *Sha'ar Tziyon*, Orach Chayim, Siman 417:2.

  2) We refrain from announcing Rosh Chodesh in order to "confuse the Satan so that it should not know when Rosh Hashanah will be, so it will not prosecute people": Levush, *Mishnah Berurah*, Orach Chayim, Siman 581:1.

  3) Since Rosh Chodesh is also Rosh Hashanah it is not fitting to say that *Rosh Chodesh* will be on such and such a day, without also mentioning that it is also Rosh Hashanah. On the other hand, if we mentioned Rosh Hashanah, it would make this month different from all other months, thus we don't mention Rosh Chodesh at all: *Aruch haShulchan*, Orach Chaim, Siman 417:9.

  4) Since Elul is always 29 days (according to the calculation of Ezra in *Beitzah*, 6a), if we know when Rosh Chodesh Elul will be, we also know when Rosh Chodesh Tishrei will be. Therefore there is no reason to announce the date.

  There are other answers as well. But all of these are relevant only if the purpose of announcing Rosh Chodesh is so that we will know its date. This is not the only reason for Birchas haChodesh. We actually

naked eye. This hiddenness represents an inner type of *Avodah* / spiritual-mental-emotional work. The same is with Yom Kippur. Yom Kippur is a more *Penimi* / internal holiday, a day of introspection, reflection and prayer. Both these holidays are celebrated mostly indoors, in the Shul, our inner space, our sanctuary. In contrast, Sukkos occurs on the full moon, the 15th day of the month, when the moon shines brightly for all to see, illuminating the landscape even when it is nighttime.

We celebrate Sukkos 'outside' our homes, under the stars. It is a time of outwardly expressed and revealed joy and dancing (The Netziv, in *HaAmek Davar*, Devarim, 16:15, writes that the language of the Pasuk regarding Sukkos is שבעת ימים תחג לה אלהיך, and thus, דבכלל לשון תחוג משמע שמחה, הבאה בריקודים ומחולות. This means that there is a special Mitzvah to dance on Sukkos. The *Tosefos Yom Tov* writes in the name of the Radak, on the Mishnah, *Rosh Hashanah*, 1:2, that תחג means 'to dance'. In general, the term *Chag* refers to Sukkos: *Temurah*, 18a-b), and even dancing in the streets, as the Rebbe strongly encouraged. It is a time of jubilant 'expression'.

Sukkos reveals outwardly what we have achieved inwardly through Rosh Hashanah and Yom Kippur. What was בכסה / hidden becomes revealed on יום הגנו, the days of Sukkos. Sukkos is a time of Simchah: the Torah tells us three times to be b'Simchah on Sukkos (*Yalkut Shimoni*, Emor 247:654), and our sages call Sukkos

---

"bless" the new month, so the question remains why don't we bless the month of Tishrei?

The Alter Rebbe once related: When I was in Mezritch I heard from my Rebbe, the Maggid, in the name of the Baal Shem Tov: The seventh month (Tishrei), first of the months of the year, is blessed by Hashem alone. With this power, we can bless the other 11 months of the year: the Rebbe, *HaYom-Yom*, 25th of Elul.

זמן שמחתנו / "the Season of our Simchah".*,* There are various types of joy which have specific terms for them in Lashon HaKodesh (there are ten expressions of joy, *Avos d'Rebbe Nasan*, 43:9), and Simchah is particularly connected to a revealed and expressed joy (Gra, on *Iyov*, 3): שמחים בצאתם / "They (the celestial spheres) are joyful when they go out (*Siddur*, Keil Adon). Simchah is a posture of "going out". Sukkos is a time when there is an outward Divine expression of what was hidden on Rosh Hashanah and Yom Kippur; the positive judgment and forgiveness of the first Holy Days is expressed outwardly in the structure of the Sukkah. On a personal level, once our inner work of Rosh Hashanah and Yom Kippur is complete, it is revealed as accepted on High in our "going out" of our homes, out into the joyful public atmosphere of Sukkos.

Rosh Hashanah and Yom Kippur are 'New Year' days, new beginnings stirring within our inner world, our desires and yearnings, our thoughts and emotions. On Sukkos these sentiments burst forth and you start actually living the new year and the 'new you'. Now you are ready and equipped to leave your inner world with expansive joy and go out into the world without fear, even in a temporary structure that a strong *Ru'ach* / wind can easily topple.

Sukkos is the great manifestation of Rosh Hashanah and Yom Kippur, the culmination and fruition of the more *Penimi* / inner Yamim Tovim; a movement from 'inside' to 'outside'. The progression of these Holy Days is not merely outward; it also moves 'deeper', and increasingly more intimate. We evolve from 'engagement' to 'marriage' to 'embrace' to 'intimacy', as explored earlier. Thus in our deeper experience, even though the Sukkah is out in the open, it is not just an outside hug; it is an intimate embrace.

ϗ
PRACTICE

RESOLUTIONS

REBBE SHALOM DOVBER, THE REBBE RASHAB, WOULD take upon himself a new *Hiddur* / beautification, a way to enhance and be more meticulous with some Mitzvah, in the beginning of every new year (*Sefer haMinhagim*, 56). A new beginning demands a new approach to life; new positive resolutions. This allows one to palpably start over again; to push the pause button on life, to rewind and begin from a higher perspective. We need to think of Rosh Hashanah not just as the birthday of humanity, a contemplation of what it means to be a part of the human race, but as our own personal birthday (as the opinion of

Rashi, who maintains that for certain issues everyone turns one year older on Rosh Hashanah, although see Rambam, *Shemos*, 30:12: ועוד קשה לי, כי מנין שנות האנשים (אינני למנין שנות עולם מתשרי אבל הוא מעת לעת מיום הולדו), a contemplation of what it means to be 'me' in particular. On your birthday it is good to spend some time with yourself and think about your life and your past, and take upon yourself new resolutions for the future (*HaYom-Yom*, 11ᵗʰ of Nisan). On Rosh Hashanah, too, we should think about our life and confirm new resolutions and projects for the coming year.

Take some time right now to consider a resolution that will focus yourself on beginning anew and rebirthing yourself. Choose a new Mitzvah to perform with more Hiddur. For example, accept upon yourself this year, and from now onwards, to concentrate more intently on the Amidah prayer or another section of Tefilah. Give more charity, or do so with a bigger smile. Learn an extra ten minutes each morning, and so forth.

Take some time to contemplate more inwardly, as well. Ask yourself penetrating questions such as:

What are your goals for this coming year?

Are you in the right place?

Do you have the job that is right for your soul's articulation?

Are you living in a balanced way?

Are you living up to your full potential?

Do you feel alive? Are you joyful?

Most of the time, for the success of the resolution, the resolution should be for small changes. Although ideally we would be able to make broad, sweeping resolutions, life is simply about orientation: am I facing upwards, am I moving upwards from where I am right now? Also, a resolution has to be realistic, something that will not be merely a flash of inspiration, later to be dropped.

It may not be sustainable to proclaim, 'From now on I will concentrate throughout the entire time I pray,' or 'I will care for my health and lose 100 pounds,' or 'I will never again become angry.' Rather, say for example, 'From now on, I will concentrate on the meanings of the words for at least ten minutes when I *Daven* / pray each morning,' or 'I will make the concrete steps necessary to lose two pounds a week,' or 'I will ensure that every day I will not put myself into a position that I already know upsets me and tempts me to flare up in anger.' Resolve to make 'small changes' in your lifestyle that will gradually better your situation. Start with small changes that you can more easily attain, and build from there. Celebrate your successes. When you feel successful in what you are doing, you will have the strength and courage to continue on, and make bigger changes.

Put your resolutions into writing in order that you can revisit them at various times throughout the year. Also write down your successes and your setbacks, and record what thoughts or reactions led you to these experiences. From time to time, reread these words, and note your progress.

KAVANNAH / MINDFUL INTENTION

In the beginning of the new year a new Divine 'exhale' of *Shefa* / influx of lifeforce flows into the world. Overall, creation occurs through Divine Speech; Hashem said, "Let there be light" and there was light. Divine speech is made up of spiritual sounds, frequencies and vibrations, which give rise to physical vibrations or energies, which in turn concentrate into matter.

The first stage of speech is an outbreath. Speech is formed when the *'Ruach* / wind' of *Hevel* / breath, passes through the Five *Gevuros* / restrictions of the mouth; the throat, palate, tongue, teeth, and lips, within a context of distinctions and meanings. By constricting and directing the flow of the exhale, these potentials of the mouth create differentiated vibrations and sounds. In this way, the root of the Divine Shefah coming into the world is like this cosmic 'exhale', and this 'wind' passes through different contractions and articulations in order to reach our conscious experience.

On Rosh Hashanah we are given the Mitzvah to 'exhale' into the Shofar and create a *Kol* / sound. This Shofar-blowing embodies and parallels the new Divine outbreath, the flow of Life force into the new year. Through the Mitzvah of blowing Shofar, we become partners in breathing the new year into existence. Yet, prior to the Divine exhale, there is first a Divine inhale, and a retention of breath. This withdrawal and retention manifests as a cosmic sense of slumber on the night of Rosh Hashanah (and during the month of Elul, as explored in *The Month of Elul: Days of Introspection & Transformation*). On the morning of Rosh Hashanah there is finally a great exhale, reinvigorating the universe. The inhale gathers up the previous year, and the exhale gives *Heviyah* / existence to the new year.

Although Rosh Hashanah is the embodiment of all the renewal that will occur throughout the entire year, the Divine inhale and exhale are actually continuous. There is a renewal of Creation every moment; new creative *Shefah* / flow fills all life at every instant, followed by a withdrawal of the old. With every Divine exhale and inhale, the life force of the world is 'running and returning'.

With every inhale, every living animal absorbs oxygen and new life force, which emanates from the Divine exhale. With every exhale, they release and empty themselves of breath and self, returning their life force to the Source of Life. As the Cosmic exhale is microcosmically inhaled, finite existence is filled with new *Chayus* / life. As the microcosmic exhale is Cosmically inhaled, finite existence flows and 'expires' back into the Infinite.

At the beginning of the New Year, focus on the new Cosmic exhale filling you and your world. As you gain awareness of the fact that this Cosmic exhale occurs every moment, you enable yourself to employ a powerful Kavanah upon awakening each morning, and any time throughout the day. Simply take notice of your breath moving in and out. With every exhale, you are emptying yourself of the old and releasing it back to Hashem. With every inhale, you are being filled with new Divine life force — new life. Breathe consciously, aware of your continual re-birthing. Recognizing this will awaken you to the opportunity of beginning anew, not just on your birthday, Rosh Hashanah, but in every moment, which is in truth absolutely new.

Next time you awaken from sleep or any time you feel the need to jump start your life, guide your awareness to your breathing. As you exhale, sense that you are not only physically releasing 'used' air, you are also letting go of all that is negative or petty, and anything that is holding you back or tying you down. Cleanse yourself of all depressing, anxiety-ridden thoughts, returning your mind to the Creator. And as you are inhaling, invite all of yourself to breathe in vitality from the Source of all Life. Open yourself to the awesomeness of becoming, in this very moment, a *Beriah Chadasha Mamash* / literally a new Creation, a new you full of new potential.

༘
SUMMARY OF TISHREI

*I*N THE MONTH OF TISHREI, THE SEASON IN BETWEEN THE
end of summer vacations and the beginning of fall and
the new agricultural year, our Avodah follows a pattern of
upward movement. To access this Avodah, we need to employ the
element of the month, *Ruach* / wind, which is an attribute of flexibility, giving us the ability to realign ourselves with the Divine and
begin a new year.

The name of the **tribe** of the month, Ephrayim, means 'fruitful',
alluding to the commandment, "Be fruitful and multiply." Yosef,

the father of Ephrayim, is fruitful even in challenging circumstances. The **verse** of the month indicates one of the principal challenges most people face: the negative Kelipah of distorted intimacy. The **sense** of the month is touch, also involving intimacy. The physical and spiritual functions of the *Marah* / gallbladder, the **body part** of the month, help us rectify our intimate lives by rebalancing our emotional and physiological systems. Ultimately, within this balance, we can elevate ourselves to the greatest sense of intimacy and unity with our Creator, and be 'reborn' into a fruitful new year. But first we must dedicate ourselves to elevating our desires back to the Source.

Tishrei, the **name** of the month, means 'to begin' or 'to dedicate', and the spelling uses letters in a backward or 'upward' flow of the Aleph Beis. The **letter sequence of Hashem's name** for this month is also a backwards or upwards flow. The **letter** of the month, Lamed, resonates with this pattern, suggesting learning, and also leaping upward beyond our seeming upper limits.

In this month, the **Torah portions** instill in us a power of renewal and rebirth, living with purpose, justice, *Teshuvah* / repentance, forgiveness and joy. These portions culminate in a celebration of the end and beginning of the Torah readings of the year. The zodiac **sign** of the month is *Moznayim* / Libra, indicating a need to re-justify and rebalance our lives. The **Holy Days** that pervade this month require us to do this, through a rigorous process of self-evaluation. This form of judgment is intense but deeply elevating, finally culminating in the celebration of our 'wedding' and intimacy with the Divine.

12 DIMENSIONS OF TISHREI	
Sequence of Hashem's Name	*Vav-Hei-Yud-Hei — moving from the 'lower' half of the Name, moving up to the 'higher' half*
Torah Verse	*VayirU osO sareI PharaoH / "The princes of Egypt saw (Sarah) — indicating the negative Kelipah of intimacy.*
Letter	*Lamed, graphically the highest letter*
Month Name	*Tishrei (the letters are in reverse flow of the Aleph Beis, below to above)*
Sense	*Tashmish / intimacy, sense of touch*
Zodiac	*Moznayim / Libra / Scales of Judgment (and balance)*
Tribe	*Ephrayim, 'fruitful even in hardship'*
Body Part	*Marah / gallbladder*
Element	*Ru'ach / wind, air, flexibility*
Parshiyos / Torah Portions	*Parshiyos of the month's Yomim Tovim / Holy Days, and the end and beginning of the Torah*
Season	*In the balance between summer and fall*
Holiday	*Rosh Hashanah, Ten Days of Teshuvah, Yom Kippur, Sukkos, Hoshanah Rabba, and Shemini Atzeres / Simchas Torah*

PART II

༃

Essays on the *Yamim Tovim /* Holy Days of Tishrei

ॐ

ROSH HASHANAH
TO SUKKOS

A Love Story

A S EXPLORED EARLIER THE MAZAL OF THE MONTH
is *Moznayim* / Libra / Scales, symbolizing the place
of balance that we want to create within ourselves,
as well as the balance between Heaven above and earth below.
In the first of the months of the year, Nisan, Hashem is reaching
out to us. It is a top-down relationship, thrusting us out of Egypt,
out of constrictions and smallness, out of negativity and enslave-
ment into freedom. We are pulled toward receiving the Torah at
Mount Sinai, even with a sense of coercion — that the mountain is
suspended over our heads. By contrast, Tishrei is characterized by
an upward flowing relationship in which we stand up and reach
out to the Reality Above. We have, by this point, become ready to

encounter the Divine in a *Panim-el-Panim* / face-to-face relationship, like a marriage or two equal sides of a scale.

The progression of the Yamim Tovim of Tishrei is the evolution of this relationship. The top-down paradigm gradually shifts into a situation in which we feel our disconnection and want a 'personal' relationship. This is the month of Elul (as explored in the volume, *The Month of Elul*). Then Tishrei initiates the engagement, marriage, Chupah, seven days of celebration, intimacy, and finally 'moving in together', or creating a dwelling place for HaKadosh Baruch Hu in this world.

During the course of Tishrei we orient ourselves into a posture of a face-to-face relationship, representing a perfect balance of the scales. Within the Zohar there is a book called ספרא דצניעותא / *Safra deTzniusa* / The Hidden Book, a very dense, intricate, and mysterious text found in the portion of Terumah. *Safra deTzniusa* begins with these words: תאנא, ספרא דצניעותא, ספרא דשקיל במתקלא. תנא, דעד לא הוה מתקלא, לא הוה משגיחין אפין באפין / "We learned in the Hidden Book, a book that was taken with a scale. We learned that until there was a scale there was no face-to-face providence." This means that if there is no balance, there cannot be a face-to-face relationship.

Each year this pattern repeats itself. Before Rosh Hashanah, we and our Creator are like Adam and Chavah in the second chapter of *Bereishis*: two separate beings in an *Achor b'Achor* / back-to-back relationship, out of touch with each other, in a state of 'distorted intimacy', so-to-speak. Cosmically, the Divine attributes of *Ze'ir Anpin (ZA)* / the Masculine Transcendent One, and *Malchus* / the Feminine Immanence, are 'facing away' from each other. On Rosh

Hashanah, the blowing of the Shofar begins the process of turning around and seeing each other *Panim-el-Panim* / face-to-face (For an in depth exploration of this topic, please see *Murmurings of Majesty: The Mysteries of Shofar & Rosh Hashanah*).

From Rosh Hashanah forward we move out of a posture of immaturity, which is like being 'attached to the hip' with HaKadosh Baruch Hu. We leave *Mitzrayim* / Egypt, the 'constrictions' of isolated, back-to-back consciousness, and enter into a state of mature consciousness in which we can be mindful, honest and responsible with our lives (this is Rosh Hashanah), ask for forgiveness (this is Yom Kippur), and finally choose to spend a full week and more, enveloped in a face-to-face Divine embrace (this is Sukkos).

Moznayim, the image of a balanced scale symbolizes this new balanced face-to-face relationship that we attain in Tishrei. When Adam and Chavah encounter each other face-to-face and are no longer attached to the hip, as it were (*Eiruvin*, 18a), Chavah (and by extension, Adam) can then be called an עזר כנגדו / 'a helper who stands opposite' her partner. This describes a genuine encounter with a real 'other', in which Adam and Chavah truly recognize each other. In this mature level of relationship, the 'other' has a healthy independence, with their own unique mind and heart, and yet they choose to be with you, a spiritual 'helper'.

Through the *Avodah* / spiritual-mental-emotional-inner work of Tishrei, we learn to stand up, to be present. We learn — from our own volition and without 'a mountain suspended above our heads' — to do Teshuvah, to become awakened, to take responsibility and ask forgiveness. We rekindle a genuine face-to-face relationship with HaKadosh Baruch Hu.

FROM BESULAH TO INTIMACY

Elul is the month that precedes Tishrei. Elul is the Mazal of *Besulah* / Virgo. Before Tishrei ensues, we prepare ourselves during the 30 days of Elul (corresponding to the transformative 30 day waiting period of the 'captive woman' in Parshas Ki Seitze, *Devarim* 21:10-14), experience the pain of our alienation and reclaim our purity, so that we can once again experience HaKadosh Baruch Hu's presence in an intimate way.

As we traverse the Yamim Tovim of Tishrei, we evolve from engagement and commitment (Rosh Hashanah), to our wedding (Yom Kippur). Then we enter the seven days of *Sheva Berachos* / feasts of the seven wedding blessings (the seven days of Sukkos), and then times of affectionate whispering and *Neshikin* / kissing (Hoshana Rabbah), and finally *Yichud* / intimate union (Shemini Atzeres / Simchas Torah).

After this entire process, we find ourselves in the month without any Yamim Tovim, Cheshvan (from the word *Chash* / quiet, as there are no holidays in Cheshvan). At this point, the 'married couple' is so fully intimate with each other, so unified in mind, heart, body and spirit, that they no longer need to look at each other face-to-face. Rather, they look forward together, sitting side-by-side, as a single unit, one in aspiration, yearning, dreaming and movement, viewing the new year that is beginning, and understanding what has to be done.

ROSH HASHANAH:
FROM BACK-TO-BACK TO FACE-TO-FACE

To move from a back-to-back to a face-to-face relationship there needs to be a severing from one another. This is clearly illustrated in the image of Adam and Chavah: "Male and female He created...." They were at first attached to each other at the 'back', one *Partzuf* / face or side being masculine and the other Partzuf feminine (*Eiruvin*, 18a). In this state it was impossible for them to recognize and appreciate each other's being, much less experience intimacy. They were both 'alone in the relationship'.

According to the Divine will, however, "It is not good for one to be alone." Therefore Hashem puts Adam (and Chava) to sleep and severs the feminine Partzuf from his 'side', i.e. his back. Out of this procedure Chavah is 'fashioned', or becomes an individual. In other words, the conjoined Adam/Chavah had to be put into an anesthetic sleep, so that they could be 'surgically' separated. Only then could they turn to face each other and recognize one another as a person. Each could then be an עזר כנגדו / a helper who stands opposite the other. On Rosh Hashanah night a supernal slumber ensues in which a cosmic *Nesirah* / severing can occur between us and our Beloved.

On the morning of Rosh Hashanah, we blow the Shofar, consciously coronating HaKadosh Baruch Hu as the Master of His universe, declaring a face-to-face relationship with our Creator. Just as "there is no King without a people," there is no love without an 'other'. Having been severed from His 'back', we are now an individual who can consciously turn around toward HaKadosh

Baruch Hu and anoint Him as our Sovereign and *Adon* / Master. We stand face-to-face with Hashem and proclaim, 'I choose You!' *Dodi Li* / "My Beloved is mine!"

This is the first step, falling in love or feeling our soul connection, and recognizing that we want to make the commitment of marriage. Such a vast decision demands serious clarity, however, and up until our meeting we must judge ourselves: 'Am I really ready to have an unswervingly honest, open relationship with my Beloved?' We are also aware that we will be evaluated and judged by our Beloved. Inwardly, we are consumed by questions: in the Creator's eyes am I prepared to be His 'partner'? Am I who I was created to be? Can I be a true human being with *Bechirah* / free choice; not living on autopilot, but making real choices in my life? What does it mean that HaKadosh Baruch Hu is giving me the Mitzvah and power to coronate Him as the King of the whole universe? Am I fulfilling His laws with love and in a way which pleases Him?

Rosh Hashanah begins a time when Hashem is *Karev* / near to us, close to each and everyone individually (*Rosh Hashanah*, 18a). It is a time when "the Source of Light is drawn to its sparks" (Mitteler Rebbe, *Derech Chayim*, p. 13d), and reciprocally, our inner Divine spark is drawn to the Source. Trembling with awe, we choose our Divine Spouse, our King.

Rosh Hashanah is thus our renewed engagement with HaKadosh Baruch Hu. Following a full 30 days of introspection, *Teshuvah* / return and reorientation, we come before Him with a mixture of trembling and confidence, dressed in our finest attire (quoted in *Tur*,

Orach Chayim, 581. *Medrash Rabbah*, Vayikra, 29). With the Shofar blasts, we declare, 'Hashem, I am Yours. Master of the Universe, I am committed to live a life with You, a life of *Chayim* / aliveness, connection, eternity, transcendence and meaning. I beseech You to inscribe me in the Book of Being Alive, into the book of *Olam haBa* / Eternity. I am passionately ready and able to live a more G-dly life, a life of deeper commitment to Torah and Mitzvos, a life of *Kiddush Hashem* / sanctifying Your Name.'

On Rosh Hashanah there is a strong presence of *Ohr Makif* / general light (also called *Makifim* / 'surrounding' lights). This means we are not focussing on the details, the technicalities of our relationship with HaKadosh Baruch Hu, rather on our general commitment. When people fall in love and commit to marry, they feel a strong bond to each other. This bond inspires and strengthens their commitment to each other in a general way — to live together, to be together for the rest of their lives — but they are not focussing on details, such as where exactly are they going to live, nor how are they going to divide the responsibilities of raising children or making financial decisions. They are in love, or they will grow into love, and excitingly decide to marry.

YOM KIPPUR:
WEDDING DAY

Next comes Yom Kippur. Chazal tell us ביום התונתו זה מתן תורה / "'On the day of his wedding' — this is the giving of the Torah." (*Ta'anis*, 26b) This is in reference to the day the Second Luchos were given, Yom Kippur (*Rashi*, ad loc). Yom Kippur is our marriage day, and thus it was once an opportune time to find a spouse.*

In Elul the process is אני לדודי / *Ani l'Dodi* / "I am to my Beloved" — we are working to get closer and closer to our Beloved. On the evening of Rosh Hashanah the Ani l'Dodi is even more pronounced, but in the morning we start shifting into ודודי לי / *v'Dodi Li* / "and my Beloved is to me," sensing Hashem's closeness.

---

* The Mishnah, *Ta'anis*, 4:8, describes maidens dancing in the vineyards on Yom Kippur, to attract attention from the unmarried men. As it is a day of atonement and forgiveness, and a bride and groom are forgiven of their sins on their wedding day (*Yerushalmi*, *Bikurim*, 3:3), this day is also dedicated to finding a spouse, as the *Yerushalmi* (*Ta'anis*, 4:11) suggests. When people are cleansed of sin, transcending egoic consciousness, as on a day like Yom Kippur, they can choose more effortlessly, accurately and clearly their fitting *Zivug* / spouse. This extends to all choices, and for this reason, certain Chassidic Rebbes would effortlessly choose an Esrog on Motzei Yom Kippur.

Perhaps the knowledge that they were forgiven is what prompted the maidens in this joyful *way of* seeking out a spouse. In the times of the Beis haMikdash, "A thread of crimson wool was tied to the door of the Beis haMikdash, and when the goat reached the wilderness the thread turned white" (*Mishnah*, *Yumah*, 6:8). When it turned white, Klal Yisrael knew they were forgiven. This is also why the maidens danced in white garments. Once there was no longer a Beis haMikdash, this joyful practice was discontinued, however, the inner dynamic remains available.

Finally, on Yom Yom Kippur, which is the 40th (today the 39th) day from the beginning of Elul, the stage of ודודי לי is complete. The numerical value of לי is 40, alluding to the completion of marriage, as the "me" and the "Beloved" are unified on the day of Yom Kippur: there is an experience of מקודשת לי / "betrothed to me".

On Rosh Hashanah we tell Hashem, 'I am committed and dedicated to You.' On Yom Kippur Hashem tells us, 'You are Mine, I hereby betroth you to Me. Let this be our wedding day.'

On Rosh Hashanah and Yom Kippur, the days of awe, we feel utterly inspired, aroused, and filled with a passion for truth and deep connectivity, for a life of Olam haBa. To some extent we all feel this during these Ten Days from Rosh Hashanah through Yom Kippur. Some may feel it for the full ten days, others mostly on the Yom Tov days, and others maybe just for a few key minutes during those 240 hours comprising the Ten Days. However, at some point during this period from Rosh Hashanah through Yom Kippur, virtually everyone who engages with it, even minimally, will have at least a few moments of sensing something deeper or more real. There is at least one experience of connection with one-self, with HaKadosh Baruch Hu, with family, community, with our ancestors, with our language, our history, or with the text of the *Machzor* / High Holiday prayer book. Whatever the sense of con-nection, these moments inspire us to live more connectedly to our Neshamah, to HaKadosh Baruch Hu, to others; to come alive.

SUKKAH:
THE CHUPAH & SHEVA B'RACHOS

Yet, inspiration is like a flame; it burns brightly for a few moments, it flashes and flickers with excitement, but without wick and oil, it is soon extinguished. General inspiration is Ohr *Makif* / surrounding light, like a flame but without the wick and oil. Even if our inspiration has led to 'falling in love', making a commitment, and even getting married — a love relationship, a marriage requires a 'wick and oil'. It demands ongoing work and practical steps of integrating the change. Therefore, at the end of Yom Kippur, Hashem says, 'I love that you are inspired to be committed to Me! Now let us wait four days before calling all the guests, the nations of the world (on Sukkos we would bring offerings corresponding to the Seventy Nations of the world), to come celebrate our seven days of Sheva Berachos, the Yom Tov of Sukkos.

We wait four days to make sure our excitement is real and authentic. Sometimes people make grand romantic gestures in the spur of the moment; they feel excited and act out their passion. But sadly, once the excitement and novelty wears off, they may even feel trapped. And so, Hashem tells us, 'It is wonderful that you are so enthusiastic and you want to be married to Me. Let us just wait a few days and see how you feel then.' Four days later, we enter the Sukkah and the celebration of our wedding, with *Yishuv haDa'as* / a settled mind (With regards to other Mitzvos there is great debate whether proper Da'as or *Kavanah* / intent is indispensable (*Berachos*, 13a. *Eiruvin*, 95b. *Pesachim*, 114b. *Rabbienu Yona*, Berachos 12a. *Tosefos*, Sukkah, 39a. *Tosefos*, Pesachim, 7b. *Shulchan Aruch*, Orach Chayim, 60. *Magen Avraham*, 3. *Beis Yosef*, Orach Chayim, 489), regarding Sukkah, the Bach (based on the words of the *Tur*)) rules that without Kavanah and Da'as the Mitzvah of sitting in the Sukkah is not fulfilled. Bach, *Orach Chayim*, 625. *Bikurei Yaakov*, 625:3).

Sitting under a canopy, under the stars, under the Sukkah, is an image of a Chupah. In this context, if Yom Kippur is the day we decide to get married, then when we sit under the Sukkah on the first night of Sukkos, we are finally under the Chupah, beginning to celebrate our wedding ceremony. We continue to sit in the Sukkah for seven days, as the days of the Sheva B'rachos, the seven days of blessing, feasting and rejoicing with the groom and bride. The Sukkah is the *Chibuk* / embrace of HaKadosh Baruch Hu, as explored earlier: the Halachic minimum for a Kosher Sukkah is two whole walls and a portion of a third wall. These three lines form the image of a chest, an arm and the shorter vector of a hand, which gather us and hold us close in an embrace. A Sukkah with four full walls is a full-body Chibuk, as it were.

Intimacy is a state of being 'present' that both transcends and encompasses time; past, present and future are all perceived to be present here and now. The spiritual intimacy of Sukkos similarly transcends and includes all time. We rest in the present, in the affectionate after-glow of Rosh Hashanah and Yom Kippur. We also dip into our collective memory of the past, gratefully remembering the Going Out of Egypt and how Hashem sat us in tents and protected us with the Clouds of Glory. Also, as we sit under the stars, we dream of the future — *Sukkah* is connected to the word סכה / to see with *Ruach haKodesh* / holy intuition (*Kad Kemach*, Sukkah), excitedly envisioning what is possible.

By going out into the Sukkah, we are declaring to our Beloved and demonstrating with our actions, 'This year, I am ready to go wherever You want me to go — even into a 'tent' or a temporary space out in the cold — so long as I will be with You.'

HOSHANAH RABBAH:
THE NIGHT OF NESHIKIN AND 'PILLOW TALK'

We moved from a back-to-back relationship to a face-to-face relationship on Rosh Hashanah morning, and realized that the One who is כנגדו / opposite us, in front of us, is an עזר / a Helper. This closeness deepens until the point that we are moved to commit to marriage, on Yom Kippur. Finally we reach the Chupah and the Divine embrace with the seven days of Sukkos. The last day of Sukkos is the mysterious day of Hoshanah Rabbah, the *Bechinah* / state or level that the Arizal calls *Neshikin* / kisses.

Sukkos is the Bechinah of the embrace, followed by Hoshanah Rabbah, the Bechinah of Neshikin, and both are prerequisites to the state of full *Yichud* / unity. Neshikin happens with the *Sefasayim* / lips, and it involves the self and the other. On the level of ultimate Yichud the self and other merge as one: והיו לבשר אחד / "They will become as one flesh" (*Bereishis*, 2:24), and this creates a third person, a child (*Sanhedrin*, 58a). Whereas on the level of Neshikin, the self is extending into the other, bridging the divide between the self and the other. *Sefah* / lip, also means 'edge', as in the *Sefas haYam* / edge or 'lip' of the sea, a place that connects the dry land with the sea. The same is with human beings; the Sefasayim are the space that connects the internal self with the external other. It is also where speech and intimate conversation emanate.

Before the full collapsing of the two as one, Neshikin unifies the upper part of the two bodies, a partial merging with the the כנגדו /

other, specifically via the mind and heart. After this there can be a healthy collapse into unity via the lower part of the body, the limbs of 'action'.

One of the prominent customs on Hoshanah Rabbah is to 'beat' the bundle of *Hoshanos* / five willow branches on the floor, as the Shulchan Aruch (*Orach Chayim*, 664:4) rules. The Gemara (*Sukkah*, 44b) speaks about taking a willow branch and חבים. Rashi (ad loc) says, this means waving it (לשון ניענוע). Yet, the Rambam understands the word חבים to mean beat on the ground or a vessel (Rambam, *Hilchos Shofar, Sukkah, Lulav*, 7:22), and that is the Halachah.

What is the "reason" for the beating, besides that it is a Mitzvah (*Yesod*) or custom (*Minhag*) of the Prophets (*Sukkah*, 44b) performed as a *Zeicher* / remembrance (*Sukkah*, 44a) of what was done in the Beis HaMikdash? On Sukkos we begin to *Daven* / pray for rain and water, and so, on the final day of Sukkos we take a willow branch which the Torah calls *Arvei Nachal* / river willows (although, technically all willows are Kosher to use, even those not grown near a river). Arvei Nachal grow near the river because they need to drink a lot of water to survive. We beat these on the floor, which releases some vapor or water from within them, symbolizing the release of water that HaKadosh Baruch Hu will hopefully 'squeeze' out of the Heavens as rains that will 'beat down' on the earth and irrigate it.

Furthermore, the Arizal teaches us (*Pri Eitz Chayim*) that the word *Aravah* / willow in its numerical value is 277, which is the same as the word *Zera* / seed (the Aravah is also analogous to Yoseph: *Midrash Rabbah*, Vayikra, 30:10. And Yoseph is connected to Yesod and Zera). Rain is like the Divine 'seed', so to speak, which impregnates the earth and all life below. In the language of Chazal, "Rain is the husband of the earth" (*Ta'anis*, 6b).

Perhaps another reason can be offered: since the willow branch (*Medrash Rabbah*, Vayikra, 30:14) represents the non-intellectual or 'simple' person of *Emunah* / faith and *Bitachon* / trust, we take it in our hands and 'beat' down the Dinim of the world, the forces of constriction and concealment (as the Arizal explains, *Sha'ar haKavanos*, hitting the ground with the Aravos sweetens the Divine attribute of judgment. See also *Zohar* 3, 31b-32a). As we are leaving the Sukkah, about to enter the larger world, we need to demonstrate that with Emunah and Bitachon we can conquer and ultimately transform the world.

Either way, in the context and construct that is being explored, the process of moving from a back-to-back posture to a face-to-face posture and then finally Yichud and intimacy with HaKadosh Baruch Hu, we see that the leaves of the *Aravah* / willow are shaped like lips (Medrash, *Ibid*). In this way, says the Arizal, the slapping of the willows on the ground is like "kissing" the ground, and it also causes the "lips" of the willow to "kiss" each other. This is the Bechinah of *Neshikin* / kissing before *Zivug* / unity, which eventually will give birth to the new year.

Perhaps it can be suggested that the vapor or water that is released through the 'kissing' of the willows is similar to the saliva that is released in the human body through Neshikin just prior to Yichud. This is one step before the release of *Zerah* / seed — and metaphorically, the release of the potential life of the new year (*Rok* / saliva and Zerah are deeply connected. Thus for Chalitzah, the woman needs to spit in order to release her bond with her husband vis-à-vis his brother: Arizal, *Sefer haLikutim*, Ki Tetze).

In Neshikin there are already beginning stages of the flow of both *Mayim Duchrin* / masculine fluids and *Mayim Nukvin* / feminine fluids. Thus, the word *Aravah*, as mentioned, is numerically the same as *Zerah*. On Hoshanah Rabba we are inching closer and closer to Yichud with HaKadosh Baruch Hu, and closer and closer to the birth of the coming year.

HOSHANAH RABBAH AS A DAY OF JUDGMENT & INTIMACY CONCEALED WITHIN THE NIGHT

Regarding Hoshanah Rabbah, the revealers of the *Sod* / secrets of the Torah teach that it is a *Yom Din* / day of judgment; it is the day of the *G'mar haChasimah* / final sealing for the new year (*Zohar* 2, 238a. *Zohar* 3, 31b. *Sefer haManhig*, Siman, 38. This is also a *Remez* / allusion to the fact that Hoshanah Rabbah — pushed forward from Shemini Atzeres, since Shemini Atzeres is Yom Tov according to the Torah, and not a time to say Tehilim, and so forth — as on a day of Din. The Korbanos of Rosh Hashanah, Yom Kippur and Shemini Atzeres, detailed in Parshas Pinchas, are all similar, thus linking all these days of Din). It is called a time of חותם בתוך חותם / a double seal (Arizal, *Sha'ar haKavanos*, Derushei Yom haKipurim, Derush 5). And this is the way it is universally practiced, as a serious day of judgment. The idea that Hoshanah Rabbah is a day of judgment similar to Rosh Hashanah is also hinted at in the *Yerushalmi* / the Jerusalem Talmud. On the verse אותי יום יום ידרשון / "To be sure, they seek Me day by day" (*Yeshayahu*, 58:2), says the *Yerushalmi*: זו תקיעה וערבה / this is the day of Tekiah (of the Shofar, meaning Rosh Hashanah) and Aravah (meaning Hoshanah Rabbah)" (*Yerushalmi, Rosh Hashanah*, 4:8). On these two days specifically, the young and old come to Shul to pray (*Pnei Moshe*, ad loc), as Hoshanah Rabbah is a serious day of Divine judgment (Additionally, since it is the day of the final judgment of water, and we need water to survive, it is thus a day of our final judgment as well. שאז גמר דין של האדם גם כן עם המים: *Bi'ur haGra*, Orach Chayim, 664).

In particular, Hoshanah Rabbah night is the most serious time of judgment. The Zohar teaches (*Zohar* 1, 220a. *Zohar* 2, 142b) and it is brought down by many Rishonim (*Ramban*, Shelach, 14:9. *Rekanti*, ibid. *Sefer Tziyoni*, ibid. *Sefer Chassidim*, 1143. *Maor v'Shemesh*, Shelach, p. 48a. *Sefer Rokeach*, 221. *Chochmas haNefesh*, p. 366. *Kol Bo, 52. Sefer haEmunos*, Sha'ar 6:4) that on the night of Hoshanah Rabbah, a person can tell by looking at his *Tzeil* / shadow in the moonlight, or lack thereof, what kind of year he is going to have and if he will live the year (the shadow of a person seems to be connected with life: *Kerisus*, 5b-6a). The Rama in Shulchan Aruch (*Orach Chayim*, 664:1) cites these Rishonim, but clearly writes that we should not pay attention to these matters, as most people do not really know what to look for in their Tzeil, and it could cause a person to think negative thoughts and even further worsen his Mazal (The moon is connected to the judgment of water, as the Bach writes, ויש להם סימן בצל הלבנה ונראה בעיני דמאחר שהלבנה מגיע יסוד המים על כן ניתן בכחה ענין זה: *Orach Chayim*, 664:1).

What is clear is that on the night of Hoshanah Rabbah there is some type of sealing of a persons 'fate', a final judgment, although of course Teshuvah can undo all decrees. There is a strong judgment on Hoshanah Rabbah night, thus there is a custom to recite *Tehilim* and read *Sefer Devarim*.

An outstanding peculiarity regarding Hashanah Rabbah is its obscurity of sources. The idea of judgment on Hashanah Rabbah is clearly delineated in the Zohar and hinted to in the Yerushalmi, but why didn't *Chazal* / the sages of the Gemara clearly teach about this? Why leave room for the skeptical minded to dismiss this notion of judgment; if judgment is so integral to Hoshanah Rabbah, why not state so clearly?

Perhaps the reason for this omission is to avoid disturbing the *Simchas* / joy of Yom Tov (as both Rav Shlomo Zalman Auerbach and Rav Chayim Kanievsky suggest). To be joyous on Yom Tov is a Mitzvah of the Torah, and Hoshana Rabbah is part of the Yom Tov of Sukkos. Knowing that it is a day of judgment may cause people to l essen their joy, and so perhaps the teachings of the serious nature of Hoshana Rabbah were kept hidden. The trouble with this hypothesis is that today everyone knows, and certain customs that mark Hoshana Rabbah as a day of judgment are even recorded in *Shulchan Aruch*. In other words, they have been public ever since the codifiers of Halachah, such as the Beis Yoseph, Rama, and Magen Avraham, began quoting Kabbalistic sources and customs. Fortunately — or unfortunately, as it may mean people are less spiritually sensitive — knowing that it is a day of judgment does not seem to tamper with people's Simchas Yom Tov.

Perhaps the reason for the omission in the Torah and the Gemara is to keep this idea as an oral transmission. Sukkos is the implementation and the progression of intimacy from Rosh Hashanah and Yom Kippur, but Sukkos is also the 'continuation' of the atmosphere of Rosh Hashanah and more specifically Yom Kippur, as will be explored further on. Yom Kippur is all about Teshuvah, following Moshe's pleas for forgiveness. It is a time when we received the second set of *Luchos* / Tablets, which was the handiwork of Moshe as a response to our Teshuvah, to *our* desiring to change. It is about the 'below', our yearning, our longing to be closer. For this reason, at the culmination of Sukkos, on Hoshanah Rabbah there are a lot of *Minhagim* / customs (also, Simchas Torah, the culmination of all the festivals of Tishrei, is all based in customs). Customs of Hoshanah Rabbah that regard it as a day of Din, include lighting extra candles like on Yom Kippur (*Shulchan Aruch*, Roach Chayim, 664:1), staying up at night reciting *Tehilim* and reading *Sefer Devarim*, eating Kreplach like on Erev Yom Kippur (the red meat in Kreplach represents Din and is surrounded by a white dumpling, representing *Chesed* / kindness sweetening our Din), and wearing a Kittel like on Yom Kippur (Rama, ibid). Torah Law is top-down; we are commanded and we follow. Minhagim, by contrast, are bottom-up; we initiate a practice in a desire to elevate ourselves and get closer to HaKadosh Baruch Hu. Perhaps this is the reason that the aspect of judgment is not stated clearly in Torah or Gemara. It should remain a living oral tradition with a sense of humanity below rising up toward Hashem.

In addition to the two possible reasons above, perhaps something deeper and sweeter is transpiring within the context of the progression from a face-to-face relationship with HaKadosh Baruch Hu, to marriage, to embrace and Neshikin.

The Bechinah of Neshikin represents a very private and quiet intimacy. Chazal tell us that there is a time during the night when the world and the home are asleep, and this is when couples gently whisper to each other (*Berachos*, 3a). This intimate whispering is where couples can transparently and vulnerably express what is really bothering them, and what they really want. There is no one else around, the doors are closed, and noise and distractions are absent. The dark of night envelops them, creating a hiding place, where the most genuine intimate dialogue or 'pillow talk' can happen. When Hashem wanted to speak intimately with Yaakov, the sun unexpectedly set before its time (*Bereishis*, 28:11, Rashi. *Chulin*, 91b). Says the Medrash, this was so that Hashem could speak with Yaakov privately. משל לאוהבו של מלך שבא אצלו לפרקים, אמר המלך כיבו את הנרות כיבו את הפנסין שאני מבקש לדבר עם אוהבי בצנעה / "This is similar to a king who is visited by his beloved occasionally, and so he declares, 'Extinguish the lanterns, as I wish to converse with my beloved one in hiddenness, quietly, privately'" (*Medrash Rabbah*, Bereishis, 68:10. On the flip side, as night is a time of hidden intimacy, Hashem even reveals Himself to Bilam during the night: *Medrash Rabbah*, ibid).

Hoshana Rabbah is our time to whisper intimately with our true Beloved, to tell HaKadosh Baruch Hu what we really want, and to be quiet together. We do not need to make any declarations or say anything aloud. We should be as lovers who have no need for formalities and externalities with each other. Thus 'no one knows' about this special day; it is not publicized in the Torah nor even in the Gemara. Nothing is said about it, as a couple does not publicize their private, intimate, one-on-one time. On Hoshanah Rabbah night, Hashem turns to His dearest ones and says, 'Tell me, what do you really, *really* want? This is just between you and Me — don't be ashamed, I am your Beloved — you can tell Me absolutely everything.'

Rav Shlomo Kluger (1785-1869) writes (*Koheles Yaakov*, Derush 7) that on Rosh Hashanah and Yom Kippur we do not ask anything for our personal selves; our requests are always for the *Klal* / the whole, the community at large: "Remember *us* for life," "Inscribe *us* into the Book of Life," and so forth. This is so we will not be, as the Zohar (*Tikkunei Zohar,* Tikkun 7) defines, hungry dogs who bark, "*Hav, Hav*" (Interestingly, there is no universally accepted sound that we use to represent the sound of dogs barking; every language and culture has a different transliteration). *Hav* in Aramaic, the language of the Zohar, means "Give!" If we are just asking, 'Give me this, give me that,' we sound like hungry dogs. This posture of refraining from personal requests is also true in formal *Tefilah* / prayer, when we are *Davening* / praying amid a crowd, Davening during the "day" which represents a time when everything is revealed. By night, however, especially at night when there is no formal dictated law to Daven, such as the hidden, mysterious night of Hoshanah Rabbah, when HaKadosh Baruch Hu beckons us into the Divine bedchamber and asks, 'My love, don't be shy, tell me all your deepest longings, your dreams (see also, *Maharsha*, Berachos, 3a, הוא רמז האשה כ"י מספרת בתפלה לבקש כל צרכה מבעלה שהוא הקב"ה). Is anything bothering you, specifically you, that you haven't been able to tell Me? I will do anything for you.'

As mentioned earlier, Hoshanah Rabbah night is associated with one's personal צל / *Tzeil* / spiritual 'shadow', and its presence indicates a good year (although, we should not pay attention to our physical Tzeil). Throughout Sukkos we sit with others in the 'shadow' of the Sukkah. The צילתה / 'shade' from the *S'chach* / permeable 'roof material' needs to be more than the sunlight. Throughout Sukkos we sit under the צל of the S'chach. We tap into the prophetic nature of the Sukkah and who we were as a people as we left Egypt and were protected by Hashem in literal booths or in the Clouds of Glory. We sit in the צלא דמהימנותא / "shadow of faith and hope" where we dream, hope, and feel what it means to be collectively protected and embraced by HaKadosh Baruch Hu. We imagine what it is for Klal Yisrael to sit in the 'Divine shade', as the Zohar teaches (*Zohar*, 3, 255b) on the verses, בצלו חמדתי וישבתי / "I delight to sit in His shade"(*Shir haShirim*, 2:3), and אשר אמרנו בצלו נחיה בגוים / "...upon Whom we said, 'He Whose shade we would live in while among the nations' (*Eichah*, 4:20)," And we visualize how it will be when the Sukkah will rise from its 'fallen' state and we will sit in the ultimate, eternal Sukkah — the collective imagination, aspiration, and *Tikvah* / hope of Klal Yisrael.

On the night of Hoshanah Rabbah, however, we are left with our very own צל — who we are as an individual, and who we can become. It is the night of our own most hidden dreams, our secret hopes and aspirations, the deepest inner yearnings of our heart.

What is our Tzeil? On a deeper level, it is a representation of our perfect image, the way Hashem imagined us to be. Every human being possesses both a *Guf Gas* / dense body and a *Guf Dak* / ethereal body (*Avodas haKodesh*, 2:26. *Nishmas Chayim*, 1:13. שבגוף ומרומז בחז״ל – חדר. כי גוף שם מקום המיוחד לנשמות העתידים להיות נולדים.רש״י נידה יג״ב. עד שיכלו וכו' – אוצר יש ושמו גוף ומבראשית נוצרו כל הנשמות העתידות להולד ונתנם לשם:רש״י. ע״ז, ה״א). The Guf Gas formation that we inhabit in this realm of existence is physical in shape and form. The Guf Dak is a more distilled and transparent version of the physical body. There are numerous names for the Guf Dak. At various times it has been referred to as the *Chaluka d'Rabanan* / garment of the sages (Zohar 1, p. 66a. *Sha'arei Kedushah*, 1:1), as a *Malbush* / garb (*Seforno*, Kavanas haTorah), and *Tzelem* / shadow, otherwise known as an 'aura' (*Nishmas Chayim*, 1:13). It is the body's prototype, the prefiguration that existed as primordial form prior to the emergence of our physical bodies.

Before the creation of the world, in the Creator's mind, in the thought of Atika Kadisha, everyone was before Him in the form that he would (eventually) receive. This is the Guf Dak as is explained in the holy books. In actuality, man was created in a Guf Gas, and his Avodah (during his life) is to attain a physical body that appears just as it appeared in the (original state of) Guf Dak. This is the Tzeil of the person that he must work on and attain during this time. This is the deepest meaning of the Night of the Tzeil.

SHEMINI ATZERES & SIMCHAS TORAH: YICHUD WITH HAKADOSH BARUCH HU

Following the seven days of Sukkos is the day of Shemini Atzeres (and in Israel this is also the day of Simchas Torah). Across the seven days of Sukkos, during the times of the Beis HaMikdash, we offered in total 70 bulls corresponding to the 70 nations of the world. On the day of Shemini Atzeres, however, we bring a single bull only, corresponding to the 'singular nation' of Klal Yisrael. Say our sages (*Sukkah,* 55b): "This is like a king of flesh and blood who said to his servants, 'Prepare me a great feast that will last for several days.' When the feast concluded, on the last day, he said to his beloved, 'Prepare me a small feast so that I can derive pleasure from you alone.'"

Intimacy demands complete privacy and aloneness with the other (אביי באלי דידבי רבא באלי פרוחי / "Abaye would even drive away flies from around his bed and Rava would drive away gnats" — so that they would not engage in intimacy in their presence: *Niddah,* 17a). Shemini Atzeres is this 'being alone with Hashem". It is a time when, as the Zohar (1, 64b) tells us, we are בלחודוי עם מלכא / "alone with the King". In another Medrash (*Tanchumah*, Pinchas, 16), a similar parable is offered in which after seven days of feasting, the King says to his beloved, נגלגל אני ואתה / "Let us roll (frolic), Me and you...." On this day we are playfully נגלגל, alone with HaKadosh Baruch Hu in true Yichud.

What began Rosh Hashanah Eve, from the cosmic slumber and the *Nesirah* / severing apart in order to move face-to-face, to the engagement, commitment, marriage, Chupah, Sheva Berachos, and Neshikin, is finally in a state of 'arrival', of Zivug and Yichud.

Atzeres comes from the word *Atzar* / stop. This simply means that we are to stop moving, as we have arrived. For weeks we were progressively moving toward Yichud, but now Yichud is present.

As explored earlier in relation to the sense of touch, Yichud or *Zivug* is a level of intimacy that demands an absence of separation and *Levushim* / garments. Rather, the contact must be 'essence-to-essence' (*Kesuvos*, 48a *Tikkunei Zohar*, Tikkun 58). For us to connect to the Yom Tov of Sukkos, there are certain Levushim or *Kelim* / vessels that the Torah tells us we need to use, for example, the *Arba Minim* / Four Species. This is similar to Pesach, when, in order to connect with the inner quality of the day, we need to eat Matzah and Maror. There is normally a need for some sort of intermediary or tool, a vessel through which to 'grasp' the *Ohr* / light and the inner quality of a given Yom Tov. On Shemini Atzeres and Simchas Torah there is nothing we need to hold in our hands, nor eat with our mouth; there are no special Kelim or Levushim needed. Without the Beis haMikdash there is no unique observance to be done on Shemini Atzeres. All we do need to do is *Atzar* / stop.

As there are no special sacred items on Shemini Atzeres, no Lulav, Matzah or Maror, there are also no *Ushpizin* / special spiritual guests that come to visit us. Each day throughout the seven days of Sukkos another Torah archetype comes to be with us; day one Avraham, day two Yitzchak and so forth. Shemini Atzeres has no items and no guests, as today is only אני ואתה / me and You, a Yichud with HaKadosh Baruch Hu without even any 'spiritual' distractions or intermediaries.

For this reason, even when we dance with the Torah on Shemini Atzeres / Simchas Torah, when we are celebrating the completion and the beginning of the new cycle of Torah reading, we do not spend extra time actually learning the wisdom of the Torah, rather we dance with a closed Torah. The Torah itself is not a Levush or separate vessel, as it is 'one' with HaKadosh Baruch Hu ("Three knots are knotted with each other, Hashem, the Torah and the People of Israel": *Zohar* 3, 73a) We embrace the Torah physically and dance with it because Shemini Atzeres / Simchas Torah is a day of essence to Essence, with no Levushim, not even the Levush of *Seichel* / intellect that is needed in the 'study' of Torah..

DANCING ON SUKKOS & SHEMINI ATZERES

Dancing is appropriate throughout all of Sukkos, not just on Shemini Atzeres / Simchas Torah. The Netziv (*HaAmek Davar*, Devarim, 16:15) writes a Chidush, that since the language of the Pasuk regarding Sukkos is שבעת ימים תחג לה' / "Seven days shall be a

Chag to Hashem" (*ibid*) thus he says, לשון תחוג משמע שמחה הבאה בריקודים ומחולות / "The word *Chag* suggests a joy that comes about through dancing" (The *Tosefos Yom Tov* writes in the name of the *Radak*, on the *Mishnah, Rosh Hashanah,* 1:2, that תחג means to dance). In the times of the Beis haMikdash there was a practice of Simchas Beis haShoeiva, where every night (besides the first night) thousands of people would gather in the courtyard of the Beis haMikdash to watch as the pious and sages would dance all night, accompanied with harps, lyres, cymbals and trumpets. Today, many do the same, with everyone participating in the dancing.

Perhaps the dancing on Sukkos also has to do with the Chupah and Sheva Berachos which Sukkos embodies — indeed, the dancing is like the dancing at a wedding.

Yet, Shemini Atzeres and Simchas Torah are saturated with dancing. There is a special *Avodah* / spiritual work of dancing. We dance with the Torah as we perform *Hakafos* / encircling the Bimah, the place where the Torah is normally read. After finishing Hakafos in the Shul where he *Davened* / prayed, the Arizal would walk home, and on the way if he heard dancing in the other Shuls, he would enter and dance along. Such is the holy Avodah of dancing on Shemini Atzeres and Simchas Torah.

As mentioned, the word *Chag* / seasonal festival, is used with regards to Sukkos. *Chag* means something that is cyclical, as in *Chug* / circle. Within the world of traditional dance, there is 'progressive dancing', dancing forward towards a destination and back again, and there is circle dancing. There is no progressive movement in circle dancing. Circle dancing is a dance of presence, of the joy of having arrived, of the bliss of Yichud.

In a circle dance there is no hierarchy, no higher or lower, further or closer, leader or follower; everyone is in a 'balance', equidistant from center, and everyone in the circle is face-to-face with the others. This symbolizes the Zivug and Yichud of Shemini Atzeres, dancing face-to-face (as humanly possible) with HaKadosh Baruch Hu and dancing with the Divine Torah.

DANCING IN THE STREET

During the seven days of Sukkos we lived enveloped by Hashem's embrace; we ate, drank, learned Torah, *Fabrenged* / participated in spiritual gatherings, and some even slept, in the Sukkah. We had nowhere else to go and nothing to do. By the time Shemini Atzeres / Simchas Torah arrives, we know very deeply that this revealed state of relationship with HaKadosh Baruch Hu is real and potentially permanent. And so we simply get up and dance. We receive the holy Torah scroll in our arms and dance. We are in love, and have arrived; our joy knows no bounds. Many of us leave the four walls of our Shul and dance with the Torah in the streets, sharing our joy with the 'outer world'. Centuries ago, there was even a custom to invite non-Jews to the Shul on Simchas Torah to celebrate with us. Our elation and songs of holiness reverberate outwards, illuminating passersby and seemingly mundane concrete structures . When a person is in love or has just achieved a big success, their enthusiasm can swell until they have an urge to shout it out on the rooftops, to proclaim to the entire universe their joy.

On this day we rejoice in our having been forgiven, in having fully accepted upon ourselves the Second Luchos and the *Torah she-b'al-Peh* / the Oral aspect of the Torah. We are so happy and in love with Hashem, it becomes uncontainable. When we dance, we defy gravity because our Teshuvah has unburdened us. We want everyone to know — not with any motive or showing off, rather because our joy is unbridled.

THE POSITION OF THE TORAH WHEN DANCING

Chazal tell husbands, "If your wife is short, bend down to whisper to her" (*Baba Metziya,* 59a). Spouses need to try to always be in a Panim-el-Panim posture, and if one's partner is seemingly not yet 'on the same level', one should 'bend down' to get into a face-to-face position. Sometimes a face-to-face relationship is between 'equals' who naturally see eye-to-eye in everything, and other times, one must 'lower' oneself to the loved one's current state of being.

The Magid of Mezritch speaks of a father who gets on the floor to play with his child. This is the idea of lowering oneself to 'reach out' and encounter the other. One's love for the other makes them willing to descend to their beloved's level of understanding. Children are naturally and mystically-speaking closer to the ground, and parents, out of their love, literally and figuratively bend down to communicate with them face-to-face.

The Be'er Mayim Chayim (Rebbe Chayim of Chernowitz, Parshas Naso) speaks of the various expressions of a parent's love for their child. Sometimes you bend down to them, but sometimes you pick up the child and hold them so that their face is in front of your own and you can look straight into their eyes. This is like a face-to-face relationship, even though it is with an immature, young child.

There are even times, when in great joy, you lift your child above your head or put them on your shoulders; you make them a 'crown' above your head. The child becomes *your* crown.

It could be said that the same applies to Shemini Atzeres / Simchas Torah, when we dance with Hashem's Torah. On Shemini Atzeres / Simchas Torah we dance holding the Torah, and become the 'legs' of the Torah. We lift the Torah and place it near our head, like a parent lifting a child up to an 'eye-to-eye relationship'. Some people, in their love and excitement, even lift the Torah above their heads. Of course we cannot literally put the Torah on our shoulders, but in many Shuls the custom is to take our children and put them on our shoulders while dancing with the Torah. This is a *Bechinah* / paradigm that is 'higher' than face-to-face, as it were, as the Torah 'crowns' us.

On Shemini Atzeres / Simchas Torah, when we finally attain the ultimate posture of face-to-face relationship, Zivug and Yichud, we may even reach a moment of 'lifting' our Beloved One, through His Torah, above our heads.

Panim-el-Panim is the objective and goal of Tishrei, the month saturated with holidays. And then comes the day after, when "Yaakov goes on his way," when we hit the road, and carry the inspiration from the Yamim Tovim into the world, empowered to transform it and create a revealed dwelling and 'resting place' for HaKadosh Baruch Hu.

BACK-TO-BACK, TO FACE-TO-FACE,
TO PANIM ECHAD / ONE FACE, ONE VISION

Up until now we have explored the paradigms of back-to-back through the highest form of face-to-face relationships. A young child's relationship with a parent is back-to-back; wherever the parent moves, so does the child. This can also be true of two mature adults, for example, when one falls in love with another because they feel overwhelmed in the other's presence, and becomes lost in them.

A more mature relationship is one of עזר כנגדו / a helper opposite him; both are independent persons, and choose to enter a relationship with the other. This is the Torah's ideal form of marriage, a face-to-face relationship. It is also the mature stage of a student and teacher relationship, or any friendship.

After a longer period of being face-to-face, the bond between the two can become so unified that they start sharing the same views and outlooks on life and even the same dreams, hopes and aspirations. Imagine a young couple sitting over a cup of tea, speaking about life and gazing at each other face-to-face. Now, imagine a more mature couple who have lived together through many years, sitting on a bench together both looking in the same direction, speaking of their shared past and dreaming of their possible shared future. There is a sense of one unified vision.

The Torah is truly Divine, being both the blueprint of creation as well as the guide that helps us live deeply with connection and purpose. Amazingly, the very first word of the Torah, בראשית, hints to these three progressive dynamics. בראשית has three vowels: the

Sheva (one dot above another dot), the *Tzeirei* (two dots side-by-side), and *Chirik* (a single dot). This reflects the levels of relationship with HaKadosh Baruch Hu; we begin with a hierarchical or back-to-back relationship, 'one dot above the other'. Then we mature to a face-to-face relationship, 'two dots' facing each other. Finally, we reach a place of looking outwards together in the same direction with the one vision, as 'one dot'.

Once the Yichud of Shemini Atzeres / Simchas Torah has taken place, it is no longer 'two' who are facing each other, rather, רצונך / your (our) will is רצונו / Hashem's will. Our wills, desires, aspirations are in total sink with, *Kaviyachol* / so-to-speak, Hashem's will. We want the same thing and thus we are ready to conquer the world. We are ready and able to go out into the world and fulfill HaKadosh Baruch Hu's desire for creation, and transform the world into a holy, G-dly place, a place where Hashem's presence is revealed and present.

ༀ

YOM KIPPUR TO SUKKOS
Floating in Space to Sacred Space

O N YOM KIPPUR THERE IS A CUSTOM TO WEAR WHITE garments, and in particular a white *Kittel* / robe. The Rama (*Shulchan Aruch*, Orach Chayim, 610:4) writes, נהגו ללבוש בגדים לבנים ונקיים ביוה״כ דוגמת מלאכי השרת וכן נוהגין ללבוש הקיטל שהוא לבן ונקי גם הוא בגד מתים ועי״ז לב האדם נכנע ונשבר / "The custom is to wear white, clean clothes on Yom Kippur, like angels. And the custom is to wear the Kittel, which is white and clean. And it is also the garment in which a person is buried, and thus (while wearing it) the heart of man is humbled and broken open."

Essentially, there are two reasons for wearing white: it symbolizes 'angels', pure and clean of negativity and sin, or it is worn as a reminder of death, in order to stimulate remorse and to humble a person's ego. These two reasons can also be seen as the two dominant themes and perspectives of Yom Kippur.

Yom Kippur is a day of forgiveness, this is clear from the Torah. The question is only how do we enter Yom Kippur, what should be our consciousness and mindset that will allow us to align ourselves with this day? Are we to think of ourselves as angels, transcendent, beyond sin, clean and white, or should we think about literally the opposite, about remorse and death? What will induce us into a Yom Kippur state of mind? Are the Mitzvos and *Minhagim* / customs surrounding Yom Kippur supposed to provoke a sense of angelic transcendence or the immediacy of death? And more deeply, what is Yom Kippur?

FROM THE FEARLESSNESS OF YOM KIPPUR
TO THE JOY OF SUKKOS

Sukkos is the revealing of the inner power of Yom Kippur and Rosh Hashanah, and their completion. The progression of Tishrei includes *Chibuk* / embrace, *Neshikin* / kissing and *Zivug* or *Yichud* / unity, as explored in the previous chapter. There are other modes of progression and unfolding, as well.

DEATH PRACTICES

When viewed as a day that pushes us into an awareness of death and the transient nature of life, Yom Kippur eventually induces a sense of fearlessness. Then, the Yom Tov of Sukkos reveals this more fully, as we fearlessly go outside and dwell in an impermanent structure, open to the elements.

Without going into great details of the prohibitions of Yom Kippur, we refrain from eating, drinking, washing, and anointing ourselves. Couples also refrain from physical intimacy and the act of procreation. These can be understood as symbols of death, and certainly the absence of furthering life.

Ceasing to eat and drink is an act of dying and death, for if we do so long enough, we will expire. The difference between fasting one day or hundred days, and thus literally passing on, is merely a quantitative difference. In essence, any fast is a miniature form of death.

Before entering Yom Kippur many have the custom of performing *Kaparos* / 'Atonements' over a live chicken. This *Minhag* / custom, which originated in the times of the Geonim, is followed by Ashkenazim who adhere to the Rama (*Shulchan Aruch*, Orach Chayim, 605:1. See also Rosh, *Yuma*, 8:23, and Tur, *Orach Chayim*, 605), and the teachings of the Arizal, in this matter (centuries ago there were other forms of Kaparos — see Rashi, *Shabbos*, 81b: ובתשובת הגאונים מצאתי שעושין הותלות מכפות תמרים וממלאין אותם עפר וזבל בהמה וכ"ב או ט"ו יום לפני ר"ה עושין כל אחד ואחד לשם כל קטן וקטנה שבבית וזורעים לתוכן פול המצרי או קיטנית וקורין לו פורפיסא וצומח ובערב ר"ה נוטל כל אחד שלו ומחזירו סביבות ראשו שבעה פעמים ואומר זה תחת זה וזה חליפתי וזה תמורתי ומשליכו לנהר. The Ramban, the Rashba, and the Mechaber, Rav Yoseph Karo, were strongly opposed to the practice of Kaparos with a chicken. Some people today use money for Kaparos and donate it to charity: *Chayei Adam*, 144:4). The basic practice is a man takes a rooster and a woman takes a hen in their hands, and they circle the bird over their head while reciting a short prayer. Following this, the bird is ritually slaughtered in front of the person, and the meat is then given to charity.

In Medieval Europe, before the industrial food revolution, the bird that was taken for Kaparos was most probably one that you raised yourself or saw your neighbor raising. There was a personal connection between you and the bird. Therefore the intention of the Kaparos, is for you, yourself, to feel the immediacy of death. In one moment, you vividly feel the aliveness of the animal in your hand, and the next moment, it is dead and being prepared to feed the poor. This 'brush with death' is meant to inspire one to Teshuvah, in the words of the Rama, עי״ז לב האדם נכנע ונשבר / "...and through that, the heart of man is humbled and broken open."

Similarly, there is a custom to immerse oneself in a Mikvah before Yom Kippur (Rosh, *Yuma*, 8:24. *Shibbolei haLeket* 283. *Manhig*, 52. Tosefos, *Berachos*, 22b. *Tur, Shulchan Aruch*, Orach Chayim, 606:4. Perhaps this is an 'obligation' and one should even recite a *Beracha* / blessing before the immersion: Rosh and *Shibbolei haLeket*, ibid). Immersion in a body of water, a Mikvah, is another 'death practice'. As with all living mammals, oxygen is essential to us, and without breathing we cease to live. Fully submerging underwater, we cease to breathe, and lack this sign of life (*Yuma*, 85a. Rambam, *Hilchos Shabbos*, 2:19. *Shulchan Aruch*, Orach Chayim, 329:4).

Immersing in a Mikvah before Yom Kippur is for the purpose of spiritual cleansing, and that is the same reason a dead body, before it is interred, is immersed in a Mikvah. This too viscerally reminds a person of death. Then, following the Mikvah, one dresses in a white garment similar to the one in which he will someday be buried.

This is one way of thinking about Yom Kippur and the state and mindset we are to be in; we are to get a sobering sense of the fickleness of life, the immediacy and eventuality of death. There is an urgency to this moment of life because it is all we have. All ambitions and drives, and all the pleasures of the world, are *Hevel* / vanity and emptiness. This is a sense that nothing is permanent, and *Sof Davar* / at the end of the day, the only thing that really matters is, as the Book of Koheles concludes, סוף דבר הכל נשמע את־האלקים ירא ואת־מצותיו שמור כי־זה כל־האדם / "The sum of the matter, when all is said and done: revere Hashem and observe His commandments. For this is the totality of man" (*Koheles*, 12:13).

Yom Kippur is a day of truth. Having, to some extent, touched 'death' and lived on its doorstep — without food or drink, and having immersed in a Mikvah and donned garments of burial — we are now able to let go of egoic fears and live life more deeply.

With an understanding that everything in this world is empty and transient, there is nothing in the world to fear. Nothing can hold us in its grip. In this paradigm, Sukkos shows us that in our fearlessness we can go outside the security, comfort and protection of our home. We can embrace the fact that this life is a 'temporary structure', like the Sukkah, and be absolutely joyful and at ease in this, sensing that we are surrounded only by the Infinite Embrace of HaKadosh Baruch Hu.

THE FOOD PIPE & THE WINDPIPE

Yom Kippur's 'death practices' — wearing a Kittel, fasting, and all the other Mitzvos and Minhagim of the day — help push us to recognize the temporary nature of life. They 'force' us to feel the urgency and the opportunity of our lifetime, and to awaken us to Teshuvah. As above, there is another function of the Mitzvos and Minhagim of the day: to lift us into a state of transcendent purity and an 'angelic' perspective.

Chazal tell us that the 365 negative commands of the Torah correspond to the 365 days of the year (*Makos*, 23b. *Tanchuma*, Ki Tetzei, 2). The Zohar (*Zohar* 1, 170a), teaches that the 365 negative commands correspond to the sinews, the main veins and arteries (or passageways) of the body. Yom Kippur is connected with the קנה / 'windpipe', the trachea.

There are two 'pipes' or passageways through which we receive fuel from the outside world into our inner world: the trachea, through which we inhale oxygen, and the ושט / 'food pipe', or esophagus, through which we ingest nutrients.

The Zohar associates the windpipe with the World to Come and Yaakov, "the man who dwelled in tents" of Torah study. The food pipe is associated with 'this world', and Eisav the hunter (*Zohar* 3, 231b). By definition, the food pipe is connected to the world of death and aggression, and the survival of the physical and egoic self. To eat we need to cut off another life, whether a fruit or an animal. Even when we eat something that has already been cut or has fallen off of its source of life, the very act of eating further cuts it away from existence; it is broken down more and more with the grinding of our teeth and processing of our stomach, and so forth. In this way life feeds off death, and the function of the Veshet, in particular, is to 'take' from life. In contrast, the windpipe merely brings in life-giving oxygen and releases carbon dioxide. This process is more peaceful and gentle, and is more about 'sharing' than 'taking'.

Since it is based in 'taking from life', the potential of the שטן / Satan, who is also the *Yetzer Hara* / negative inclination and the *Malach haMaves* / Angel of Death, resides with the ושט / *Veshet*. When a person overeats they over-use their Veshet. For example, when one eats too much bread ("eating bread" is sometimes used as a metaphor for indulging physical pleasures for their own sake), one ends up sinking lower and lower into the world of שטן, of the *Yetzer Hara* / ego-driven reality.

שטן and ושט have similar letters, sharing the Shin and Tes (שט). The dissimilar letter is the ו of ושט / *Veshet* and the final Nun, ן of שטן. The ו and the ן are graphically almost aligned, the only difference being that the ן extends further down, below the baseline. Through overeating, says the Zohar (Ibid, see also, Shaloh, *Sha'ar haOsyos*, Os Kuf, Kedushas haAchilah, 232), the ו descends and *Veshet* becomes *Satan*.

שטן is also related to the word שטות / *Sh'tus* / foolishness (*Shaloh*, ibid), which refers to the trivial temptations of the fleeting, transient moment. Momentary 'satisfaction', if it can be called satisfaction at all, is what causes a person to sink lower and lower and further and further from his or her true self and become enmeshed in the Yetzer haRa and the Angel of Death. Indeed, as the Rambam emphasizes, overeating can lead to health issues that shorten one's life. Besides being a metaphor for materialism, overeating is a gateway to other materialistic indulgences and compulsions.

We are meant to 'take' from life in a balanced way, not to deny our physical and psychological needs. We are meant to consume fuel and resources, to be married, to work in this world, to 'take in' and digest elements of the world with the power of our Veshet. Although, to create balance, as we receive from life we need to give even more back. If taking becomes dominant and we begin to become obsessed and then possessed by the need to take and have more and more, and we sink lower and lower. And then, instead of a Vav we have a Final Nun. A Vav descends, but stays above the baseline, within the borders of a healthy ego and a balanced fulfilment of instinctual needs. A Final Nun descends below the baseline of what is healthy, degrading our lower instincts in an attempt to satisfy bottomless desires.

"Rav Yochanan said, 'A man has a small organ (used for physical intimacy), if he starves it (does not overindulge), it is satiated. If, however, he satiates it (and overindulges), it starves, and desires more" (*Sukkah*, 52b).

Physical desire belongs to a world of 'incompleteness' and is by nature insatiable. In fact, the more one tries to fill a physical desire — the more he "satisfies" it — the more it "starves" and craves fulfillment. Attempting to fill a sense of lack only creates more lust for its object, in a loop or 'self-fulfilling prophecy' of ever-greater lack. Trying to fill emptiness creates greater emptiness, because every time a desire is satisfied, the 'vessel' of that desire expands. As the vessel expands, so too does the 'empty space' within it, along with feelings of emptiness and dissatisfaction.

Such is the nature of *Olam haZeh* / this world, the realm where the Veshet is dominant and the "hunter, Eisav" rules supreme. We have to be vigilant that the 'taking' of the healthy Veshet does not become imbalanced and fall below the line into the abyss of the emptiness and transience of the outer world, the realm of Satan, the Yetzer haRa, and ultimately the Angel of Death.

YOM KIPPUR AS ANGELIC, LIGHT, AIR — THE DAY OF THE קנה / WINDPIPE

Chazal / our sages tell us (*Yuma*, 20a) that the word השטן / the Satan is numerically 364, as the Satan has sway during 364 days of the year, excluding the 365th day, which is Yom Kippur. Throughout Yom Kippur we have no connection to the world of Satan, nor to the actual Veshet for that matter, as we literally do not feed our physical cravings.

Yom Kippur is the day of the 'windpipe', when we are nourished only by breathing and praying. Yom Kippur is the day of *Ruach* / spirit, and the day of *Neshamah* / soul. *Neshamah* comes from the word *Neshimah* / breath. We demonstrate that we do not *essentially* rely on food, rather, we live off breath and spirit. The Arizal teaches (*Eitz Chayim*, Yom Kippur) that on Yom Kippur, Malchus, which is also a code word for our reality, receives its food directly from Binah, which is called the *Hevel HaElyon* / the Supernal Breath.

On Yom Kippur we are like angels who exist without food, drink or procreation. We don white garments to symbolize that we are as pure as angels, following our immersion in the life-purifying Mikvah. We are transcendent and bright.

Angels are 'creatures of the wind', weightless and unburdened by the gravitational pull and burden of sin and negativity (King David says, "For my iniquities have overwhelmed me; they are like a *heavy burden*...." *Tehilim*, 38:5). We are released from all burdens on Yom Kippur and fly upwards like angels. Many even have the custom to stand, as much as possible, while praying on Yom Kippur, embodying an angelic posture, upright and reaching upwards.

Many people feel physically lighter on Yom Kippur, perhaps like floating above the world, certainly during the later hours of Yom Kippur. We are detached from the downward pull of the Veshet and food, and all the things that can make us feel heavy and degraded in our lives.

It can be said that we do not 'fast' on Yom Kippur at all, rather, we are 'free' from food, from drink and intimacy. This is a 25-26 hour time period when we are free of the *Bechinah* / paradigm of the Veshet and nothing can hold us down or even bring us down.

We begin Yom Kippur with the Kol Nidrei service. Without getting into the details, the basic function of Kol Nidrei is the annulment of our vows. How exactly this works, and which vows are annulled, and why should we annul vows and commitments, is for another discussion. But let it suffice to say that annulling vows is a way of letting go of attachments. We begin Yom Kippur by becoming free of the Veshet, and of ourselves, so to speak.

Similarly, the tractate that deals with the laws and practice of Yom Kippur, *Yuma* / The Day (as it is "the one unique day" within the 365 days of the year), begins this way: "Seven days prior to Yom Kippur, the *Cohen Gadol* / the High Priest would be removed from his home" (*Yuma*, 1:1). The same Mishnah teaches us that for the Cohen Gadol to serve on Yom Kippur he must be married and his wife must be alive. And yet, he is removed from his wife and from his home, even seven days prior to Yom Kippur. He then returns back home, in great joy, after he concludes the last service that he performs on Yom Kippur. He is married, but 'separated', meaning detached, from his wife, home and family life. The Cohen Gadol needs to be a family man, yet, to prepare for Yom Kippur, he also needs to become 'free' from his identity as a worldly person. He needs to be a person who is, throughout the year very grounded in the world of Veshet, but on Yom Kippur he needs to be a person of the Kaneh, as free as the whirling wind, a person of *Ruach* / spirit and *Neshamah* / soul and Supernal Breath.

As we pass through the gate of Kol Nidrei, we are similarly untied from the world of physicality and the needs of the ego, and we are lighter. Like the Cohen Gadol, we can now soar into the higher realms of purity and light.

On Yom Kippur we ask HaKadosh Baruch Hu for סליחה / forgiveness. The root of the word סליחה is, perhaps, לח / dampness, moisture. Having been stuck in a hardened negative pattern of behavior, with actions that pull us down and make us spiritually parched, we ask Hashem to free us, and make us moist and softened with the pure dew of Heaven. All sin and negativity, that may have clinged to our mind and body from our past actions, slides off us so we can start over again, fresh and light. Yom Kippur is a day of atonement and forgiveness, of liberation from our past and our negative actions and mindsets. We begin anew, perfectly clean, like a freshly laundered white garment.

YOM KIPPUR & THE WINDPIPE
VS. TISHA B'AV & THE SCIATIC NERVE

As mentioned, Yom Kippur is a "full day fast" of 25 to 26 hours. The other full day fast of the year is the fast of *Tisha b'Av* / the Ninth Day of the Month of Av. Yom Kippur is connected to the windpipe, and the only other day of the year that the Zohar reveals as being connected to a body part is Tisha b'Av. Tisha b'Av is connected to the *Gid haNasheh* / sciatic nerve, and the Mitzvah to not eat this nerve (*Zohar* 1. p. 70b).

In the verse, "Therefore the Children of Israel do not eat את גיד הנשה / *Es Gid haNasheh* / The dislodged vein", the word את / *Es* / the (spelled Aleph-Tav) is a reversed acronym for *Tisha Av* / the Ninth of Av (*Akeidas Yitzchak*, Vayishlach, Sha'ar 26). Furthermore, the numerical value of the words את גיד הנשה / *Es Gid haNasheh* is the same as the words *Tisha b'Av* (Rebbe Pinchas of Koretz, *Imrei Pinchas*, p. 7).

The Gid haNasheh is a part of the animal that we do not eat; in fact, we must completely remove it. The Gid itself has no taste, as our Sages teach: *Ein Gidim Nosein Ta'am* / nerves do not transmit taste (*Chulin*, 101a. Tur and Shulchan Aruch, *Yoreh De'ah*, 100). The sciatic nerve represents *Cheser* / absence, on every level. It even has a Cheser in its utility for us in that we must not eat it: "Therefore the Children of Israel do not eat…" It has an existential Cheser, as it must be eliminated, and it has a sensorial Cheser, as it is tasteless.

Tisha b'Av is all about Cheser, absence, mourning the destruction and absence of the Beis HaMikdash, and feeling our loss. The abstention from eating on Tisha b'Av is connected to the mourning for the Cheser in the world. As the Berditchever, Rebbe Levi Yitzchak, once *Krechtzed* / sighed on Tisha b'Av: "Who *could* eat on this day!" This is much like when a person is in a place of mourning and feeling Cheser, the void in their life, they lose their appetite, and cannot eat even if they wanted to do so.

Yom Kippur is not about Cheser, it is about transcendence. It is not about refraining from eating, rather being beyond eating. Yom Kippur is a time of the windpipe; food and eating are irrelevant to us, as the Berditchever continued, "and on Yom Kippur who even *wants* to eat!" We are beyond being anchored by food, and for that matter, all physicality. None of it is an issue for us. We are simply borne aloft, breathing in the ever-pure Supernal Breath.

SUKKOS AS A TIKKUN AND GROUNDING OF YOM KIPPUR

On Yom Kippur we un-hinge ourselves from the stuckness of negative attachments, to sin and mindsets that pull us down, and we become free 'air people', flowing like the wind of הבל / *Hevel* / breath, soaring in the Divine *Ayin* / emptiness. We are liberated from the influence of the Veshet / esophagus and all its associated *Yeshus* / limited being, and attachment to physical hungers.

We are lighter, less anchored in the 'animal self'. We are 'nourished' from the Supernal Breath of HaKadosh Baruch Hu alone (*Kaviyachol* / so-to-speak). All we need is to breathe and 'be breathed'.

We taste a state that is expressed by Shelomo haMelech in the beginning of the Book of Koheles: הבל הבלים אמר קהלת הבל הבלים

הכל הבל / "*Hevel Havalim* — Emptiness of emptinesses, says Ko-heles, emptiness of emptinesses, everything is empty" (1:2). Despite this statement, Shelomo haMelech did not descend into a sense of futility in the transient nature of existence. Rather, he concludes the book with the word, –סוף דבר הכל נשמע את־האלקים ירא ואת מצותיו שמור כי־זה כל־האדם / "The sum of the matter, when all is said and done: revere Hashem and observe His commandments. For this is all of man" (*Koheles*, 12:13). Without embracing this profound spiritual instruction, a person who has recognized the emptiness of this world (the seven "Havalim" in the previous verse, corresponds to 'this world': *Zohar* 1, 146b. There are seven mentions because the world of Havalim was created in seven days, through the seven lower Sefiros) may end up in a vacuum of meaninglessness and purposelessness with no desire for anything, even for spirituality, Torah or Mitzvos.

However, standing in *Hevel Havalim* for the 25 to 26 hours of Yom Kippur is essential to allow a deep unhinging and unbinding from negativity. It allows everything external to our souls and deeper purpose to slip away. The spiritual danger is when the *Hevel* modality becomes so dominant that we lose our sense of purpose and value all together. Some people may become swept up in the *Ayin* / no-thing-ness of existence that they lose their footing in this world.

Without being able to say, סוף דבר הכל נשמע / "The sum of the matter, when all is said and done, is: revere Hashem, observe the Mitzvos," a person can get lost in the abyss of nothingness. One senses merely that הכל הבל / everything is no-thing. One loses all desire, drive, yearning and dreaming (however, when firmly joined with reverence of Hashem, Mitzvah observance, and proper spiritual yearning, the ongoing realization that הכל הבל / everything is no-thing is an essential element to our full actualization of the path of Torah.)

This is yet another reason why Sukkos follows Yom Kippur. Even during the four days between Yom Kippur and Sukkos, "The entire nation is busy doing Mitzvos; one is engaged with building his Sukkah, another is busy arranging his Lulav...." (*Medrash Rabbah*, Vayikra, 30:7). This grounds our realization of 'emptiness' in positive, reverent actions, making it transformative. Sukkos completes Yom Kippur.

On Sukkos, HaKadosh Baruch Hu carves out a *Makom* / space for us in this transient world. Hashem says to us, 'You feel emptied and untangled from your old ego-driven identity, that is beautiful!' And if because of that emptying you cannot find your 'space' in the world, come into My Sacred Space (כשם שחל שם שמים על החגיגה כך עצי סכה אסורין. This includes the walls as well. :חל שם שמים על הסוכה *Sukkah*, 9a. כל שמונת ימי החג בין עצי דפנות בין עצי סכך: Rambam, *Hilchos Sukkah*, 6:15. At least the walls that are essential to Sukkah: Tosefos, *Sukkah*, 9a. The Rosh, however argues). Come, build yourself up again, in a gradual, healthy, holy, wholesome way.'

Although it is a temporary structure, in the sacred space of the Sukkah we are given the ability to rebuild our sense of self and begin to carve out a space for ourselves within this world. Indeed, after being in a Sukkah for seven or eight days, we re-enter the more permanent space of our homes, both literally and metaphorically.

When we are 'air people' we cannot be located within the walls of a permanent home. Therefore the Torah tells us, 'Come into My Space, this temporary, wind-blown 'home'; come, settle here for a time and find your 'footing' again.

We progress from borderless 'air' to a temporary, permeable structure, to a conventional home with strong walls and a roof. This is because for an old *Yesh* / mode of existence to become a new Yesh, it must be stripped of 'existence' and pass through a stage of *Ayin* / no-thingness, as in 'becoming air'. However, it is equally necessary to 'return' to a state of Yesh, to ground the new Yesh in the world.

On Yom Kippur we strip ourselves from our selves, as it were, divesting and transcending all attachments to this world and even our survival (without food / drink). We live in an ambitionless, dreamless, pastless and perhaps even futureless space, stripped of all 'surface' identity. Sukkos is a time to reintroduce ourselves to selfhood — this time, a healthy, holy, wholesome self, a self with positive and holy ambitions, dreams and desires.

To return to selfhood, we first enter a ephemeral, somewhat 'airy' space, Hashem's Space. There, we start to feel comfortable and embraced, protected and shielded by the Divine hug. And here we begin to dream again.

Sitting in the Sukkah under the vast sky, with the stars peeking through the S'chach, we feel our lives are returning to us. We begin to once again be filled with hopes, dreams and excitement of all the possibilities for the coming year and the rest of our life.

A state of *Hevel* / self-emptiness is absolutely freeing, but if it becomes stagnant, it can also end up being depressing, as nothing seems to be worthwhile, nothing is meaningful, and there is no real 'reason' to exist. *Ye'ush* / giving up, surrendering into depression can be a negative consequence not only of being mired in Yesh, but also of being stuck in a Hevel modality. And so, Sukkos comes along to bring us into a grounded, healthy, holy, wholesome fullness. With gratitude, we find a new space for ourselves and our lives, and suddenly the joy of life returns — we now feel full of possibility and vision.

Sukkos is זמן שמחתינו / a time of our joy, our regaining the joy of being. Sukkos is also חג האסיף / the Festival of Ingathering, literally meaning the end of the harvest period. Inwardly, this means 'the time of self-gathering', in which we collect and reintegrate our 'self' which we had transcended.

S'CHACH AND THE WORLD OF POSSIBILITY

Following the 'death practices' of Yom Kippur, we immediately begin to return to life, and to fill our lives with positive, holy and meaningful content, dreams and yearnings.

In the Sukkah we sit under the S'chach, which represents a higher or deeper realm called *Olam haMalbush* / The World of Garment (Gra). In the most simple description, Hashem, the Infinite One, creates the world (and all worlds) using the 22 letters of the Aleph-Beis. The primordial sounds of the Aleph-Beis are the vibrational building blocks of this and all universes. Everything is created by a combination of Divine sounds, which continue to vibrate and sustain existence with a Divine pulse. The micro- and macro- movements of everything in the world are manifestations of corresponding spiritual movements and vibrations emanating from the stillness and Oneness of the *Ohr Ein Sof* / Infinite Light. These vibrations or letters are the very first 'movements' rippling out from within the *Ohr Ein Sof* / Infinite Light.

The first revealing of the Divine desire to create is in the *Olam haMalbush* / World of the Garment. This 'garment' is composed of the 231 possible Hebrew letter combinations. Since there are 22 basic letters in the Aleph-Beis, combining each letter with another creates 462 combinations (22 letters x 21 letters = 462). Out of these 462, there are 231 possible 'forward combinations' of letters, also called *Panim* / face-combinations, such as Aleph-Beis, Aleph-Gimel, Aleph-Dalet, etc. — and 231 backward combinations, also called *Achor* / backward combinations, such as Beis-Aleph, Gimel-Aleph, Dalet-Aleph, and so forth.

These primary letter-compounds are the supernal 'sound-bank' from which all sound, vibration, frequency, energy and matter emerge. This sound-bank houses the vital potential to reveal the Infinite Light and then the finite vessel of Creation.

This World of Malbush is the world in which we sit on Sukkos. Sitting under the S'chach means being present in a world of 'all possible combinations'. We are sitting embraced by the Infinite creativity of HaKadosh Baruch Hu, in which everything is possible. In this embrace we are given the ability to recreate ourselves anew, to find new possibilities and to locate ourselves in a new, healthier, holier space in this world.

Our groundedness that is revealed on Sukkos, our holy longings and dreams, are predicated on our self-transcendence on Yom Kippur. However, it should be clear that as Hashem has placed us in this body and in this world, the Divine objective is not for us to continue to live like *Luft Mentchen* / 'air people', in the world of the windpipe, with zero attachment to anything related to this world. Our ultimate purpose is not to be like angels as on Yom Kippur, with no ambitions, dreams or desires — but to be above this world and simultaneously in it. Achieving this paradoxical posture allows us to transform the very fabric of this world into a world of peace and justice, of righteousness and charity, of holiness and Divinity, a place saturated with Torah, Mitzvos and "reverence for Hashem".

JOY & MOVEMENT / GROWTH

Sukkos is an antidote to the potential Kelipah of depression and nihilism that may come from remaining too long in the transitional state of Hevel.

Sukkos, as explored earlier, is a time of Simcha. The word שמח / *Sameach* / happy is similar to the word צמח / *Tzemach* / 'sprout' or plant (Shin and Tzadik are interchangeable. For example, יצחק is spelled ישחק in *Tehilim*, 105:9). Our joy returns to us when we are once again sprouting, growing and aspiring, when we are reaching upward toward our purpose, flowering in our talents and bearing fruit in our inner qualities.

NIGHT OF THE צל AND צלתה מרובה מחמתה

Sukkos is the time to regain and revitalize our aspirations and dreams. As explored earlier and brought down in the Rishonim, on the night of Hoshanah Rabba a person's צל / *Tzeil* / shadow tells him or her whether he and his family will live the coming year and what kind of year he will have. In this way, Hoshanah Rabba night, the final night of Sukkos, is the 'Night of the Tzeil'. On Sukkos we need to sit in a Sukkah where צלתה מרובה מחמתה / "The shadow from the S'chach is more prevalent then the sunshine that comes through the S'chach." We too need to be in a place where there is 'more צל than sunshine'.

Sun represents predictability and rigid inevitability, as it rises and sets in the same way each day. The sun is always full in the sky, even behind clouds. It is always the same. For this reason, "There is nothing *new* under the sun" (*Koheles,* 1:9). On Sukkos we need to make sure that there is always more Tzeil than sun, that we sense sitting in בצלו חמדתי וישבתי / "I delight to sit in his shade" (*Shir haShirim,* 2:3). We need to sit in a condition that has more inner flexibility, imagination, and openness to new possibilities, than belief in static, empirical or inevitable structures or realities.

A Sukkah is a manifestation of the attribute of Malchus (as the Rekanti writes on Parshas Emor, in the name of the Ramban), it is a temporary, transient structure, as Malchus "has nothing of its own". Sukkah is called a מצוה קלה / "light Mitzvah" because לית ביה חסרון כיס / "Performing it involves no monetary loss" (*Avodah Zarah,* 3a). "A light Mitzvah" also indicates the Sukkah's connection to Malchus (Rav Yaakov Sekili, a student of the Rashba, *Torah haMincha,* Derasha 3, although, he speaks about the element of Malchus that does not lack anything). The state of the 'Sukkah' of Malchus is always in flux; sometimes it is a *Sukkas haNofeles* / "Fallen Sukkah", and sometimes a *Sukkas Shaleim* / "Complete Sukkah" not associated with any 'loss'. As the vessel of the Sukkah "has nothing of its own", it gives us the opportunity to fill its 'empty space', and fill our own inner empty spaces with aspirations and hopes.

Inwardly, צל / 'shadow' refers to our subconscious mind, our innermost dreams. On Sukkos we need to sit in this deep realm of imagination and reveal our subconscious, envisioning and building up a healthy and holy *Tzurah* / image of self. This Tzurah is a reflection of the צלא דמהימנותא / the shadow of faith, which is an epithet of the Sukkah (*Zohar* 3, 103a). The new self that we are creating is composed of faith in HaKadosh Baruch Hu, the Creator of all Life, and faith in oneself as well — faith in our dreams.

This new *Tzurah* emanates from within the emptiness of form and attachment that is attained on Yom Kippur, from within the 'transcendence' and 'death' of Yom Kippur. (The Halacha is that if someone does not see a friend of his for one year, he should recite "Blessed is the One who resurrects the dead." This is because, as the Marasha, *Chidushei Agados,* Rosh Hashanah, explains, having gone through Rosh Hashanah and Yom Kippur, a time of judgment for life and death, it is as if one has been resurrected from the dead: *Orach Chayim,* 225, *Mishnah Berurah* 4). We are carving out a new space for ourselves, and sitting in the Infinite expanse of the World of Malbush. Now it is clear to us that everything is possible.

By the night of Hoshanah Rabbah we have sat in the Sukkah, under the S'chach, for six days. We have built ourselves up again, re-established and reconfirmed our most wholesome aspirations for the coming year. From Rosh Hashanah, our collective 'birthday', through Yom Kippur when we tuned into the deepest Teshuvah that HaKadosh Baruch Hu makes available to us, we were radically rebirthed. We began weaving our 'garment' of *Makifim* / Surrounding Light and dreams, dwelling within the cosmic Sukkah in the World of Malbush.

Now it is the night of Hoshanah Rabbah, the night of the צל / *Tzeil*. Tonight we need to go out and 'check our Tzeil' (though not literally: the Rema), and observe — have we built up our human hopes and longings sufficiently? If we cannot see our Tzeil on this night, if it is not defined and clearly revealed, we could sink into the negative side of *Hevel* / transcendent self-emptiness, and end up 'dying', so-to-speak (and even a metaphorical or spiritual death can eventually manifest as literal death, although we should not pay attention to this or ruminate about it).

If we do not emerge from Yom Kippur and the days of Sukkos with a positive Tzurah / form and posture of hope for the future, then, G-d forbid, we may end up being swallowed in the vast, luminous *Bitul* / self-nullification of Yom Kippur, outshining all our shadows. If we do not filter this light and reconnect with the romance of earthly life, our creativity and drive for life may end up 'passing away'. We need to let go of being an angel and make sure we see the beautiful 'shadow' cast by our opaque earthly self.

NEGATIVE HEVEL: LIVING AS AN IMITATION

The Torah describes two children of Adam and Chavah: Kayin / "Cain" and Hevel / "Abel". It is a tragic tale, in which due to raging jealousy, Kayin kills Hevel. The story opens with Kayin, the farmer, feeling inspired and desiring to bring an offering to Hashem — albeit, not from his best produce. Hevel sees what his brother is doing, and he imitates, but brings the best offering he can. Hevel's offering is accepted on High and Kayin's is not. Overwhelmed by envy, Kayin kills Hevel.

Clearly, Kayin was responsible for the murder. Yet, from a deeper perspective, Hevel was already "a broken vessel that was broken"; he was spiritually dead before he was killed. His physical death was just an outward manifestation of what was already happening inside. When Hevel saw what his brother initiated, Hevel was suddenly swallowed up into the Kelipah of *Hevel* / emptiness, the world of *Ye'ush* / letting go, giving up. He was no longer inspired, and he stopped aspiring towards originality; he merely became an automaton: והבל הביא גם־הוא / "and Hevel, he too brought" (*Bereishis*, 4:4). He was merely copying his brother. He happened to bring his most expensive possession, but it was not sincerely brought from his heart or inspired by a love of life. He no longer saw the value of himself as a unique individual. A person who stops living authentically stops dreaming and ends up merely imitating what others do.

This is what we need to check ourselves for on Hoshanah Rabbah night: Is our Tzeil observably vibrant and filled with a desire to express our authenticity and uniqueness? Or have we not yet returned from our 'death practices' of Yom Kippur, and are only 'imitating' our human aliveness? We still can *Chap Arein* / 'seize the moment' during this powerful time of Hashanah Rabbah, the time when the 'final sealing in the Book of Life' for the coming year is taking place. We can still begin to dream of what we will accomplish in this lifetime. This is the *Omek* / depth of what it means to 'see your Tzeil' on the night of Hoshanah Rabbah.

THE UN-TYING OF THE LULAV

Torah reveals that on Sukkos (essentially on the first day), we need to take "the product of Hadar tree and כפת תמרים / branches of palm trees" (*Vayikra*, 23:40). For the first six days of Sukkos we need to ensure that our Lulav, the branches of the palm tree is כפ / tied together as one. In the words of our sages כפות תמרים, כפות אם היה פרוד יכפתנו / "(Regarding the) branches (כפת) of palm trees: כפת (means 'bound', indicating that) if the leaves of the Lulav were spread, one should bind them" (*Sukkah*, 32a). For this reason, to ensure that the Lulav always remains 'bound', the custom is to place five ties distributed across the length of the Lulav, or to employ one of the other customary ways of binding the Lulav.

This is for the first six days of Sukkos. On the seventh day, on Hoshanah Rabbah, the Tur and Shulchan Aruch (*Orach Chayim*, 664) rule that we should undo (at least some of the) ties on the Lulav, and that it should not be so כפות / tied together.

The Mordechai (in *Lulav haGazel. Tur, Beis Yoseph*, ibid, 664) brings down in the name of earlier Rishonim (also written in the *Rokeach*, Siman 220), that since in the Torah the words כפת תמרים / branches of palm trees is missing a Vav (as the word כפות / tied is with a Vav), this omission hints to us that for six days the Lulav should be כפות tightly tied together, but on the seventh day, Hoshanah Rabbah it should be untied, at least slightly.

One simple reason for untying the Lulav is so that it can be waved more freely, which creates more joy (*Levush*, Orach Chayim, 664). Additionally, since one purpose of waving the Lulav in all four directions is the negation of negativity — "to counter the harmful winds, and up and down to counter harmful dews" (*Sukkah*, 37b) — on the day of the "final seal" we shake and wave the Lulav more vigorously and get rid of all negativity (*Bach*, Orach Chayim, 664:2).

In the context of Sukkos following Yom Kippur, which again is the building of a healthy, holy Tzurah / form following immersion in the formlessness and emptiness of Yom Kippur, the unbinding of the Lulav represents an inner loosening that can only come with a confirmed identity and strong Tzurah. Having established a positive posture and Tzeil, and having secured this newfound identity, on Hoshana Rabbah day we can unbind the Lulav and let it wave and shake with less restraint.

Only a person who is secure in his or her identity can afford to relax in this way. The more comfortable a person is with himself, the more he can take himself lightly. When a person is fighting to find who they are in this world, struggling to establish an identity, there is little room for flexibility or humor. A person with an unhealthy, fragile ego is not malleable enough to make light of himself. Only when, like an anchor, you are solidly rooted in yourself, there is room to shake and wave in all directions, to let loose without losing your center and core integrity. A healthy, holy Tzurah is more open and able to be released from imposed restraints.

Hoshana Rabbah leads into Shemini Atzeres / Simchas Torah, a time when we dance with the Holy Torah. It is because our identity is now so secure, we know so deeply who we are, our Teshuvah is so complete, our re-acceptance of Torah is so ingrained, and we are so grounded in our real dream and purpose of living, that we can jump and dance and lift off the physical ground. Like an unbound

Lulav, we can freely move up and down and in all directions. Our identity is so completely unified with the Torah, that we can now dance and move freely, effortlessly and with ease, in all dimensions.

༜

YOM KIPPUR
From Forgiveness to Joy

*A*FTER 25 OR 26 HOURS OF INTENSE *DAVENING* / praying, self-reflection and *Teshuvah* / turning ourselves toward the Infinite One, after the day dedicated by the Torah as a day of atonement and total forgiveness, after we have stood in an angelic posture and state of consciousness for the entire day, the first words we utter as we begin the *Ma'ariv* / evening service directly after Yom Kippur are עון יכפר רחום והוא / "May the All-Compassionate One forgive our sins!" What sins are we mentioning? We have just been completely purified of all sins and their effects; what could have possibly been done in the short moment between the conclusion of Yom Kippur and the beginning of Ma'ariv?

While no sins were done, for there was literally no time to act at all, a terribly devastating thought may have crossed your mind. In the split second between Yom Kippur and Ma'ariv there is just enough time to entertain the thought: Did it really work? Have I really been forgiven? Having gone through the gut-wrenching, soul-bearing, body-transcending day of Yom Kippur, the greatest sin in the world would be to feel that maybe your efforts on Yom Kippur were a waste, maybe forgiveness was not granted. For this tragic sin we cry out, "May the Merciful one, forgive our sins". Forgive us, any of us, who think for a moment that we were not forgiven. Forgive us for being so down on ourselves and for doubting You.

After Yom Kippur we ought to feel elated, light, open and cleared of all negativity. As Yom Kippur comes to a close a Heavenly Voice rings out לך אכול בשמחה לחמך ושתה בלב טוב יינך כי כבר רצה האלקים את מעשיך / "Go your way, eat your bread with joy, and drink your wine with a merry heart; for G-d has כבר / already accepted your works" (*Koheles*, 9:7). For this reason, the night following Yom Kippur we eat and celebrate joyously (*Shulchan Aruch*, Orach Chayim, 624:7). After a full day of Yom Kippur we need to sense that כבר רצה / Hashem has already accepted on High our *Tefilos* / prayers and we are forgiven, we are free. There is a sense of כבר / "already" — we are already in a posture of wholeness, lightness and holiness.

If you sense a certain lightness of being or that you have been freed of the weight of your past actions, this is not merely because you did not eat for 25 hours, rather, it is a symptom of something deeper. You have indeed been forgiven and atoned; our Creator says with complete clarity, כי ביום הזה יכפר עליכם לטהר אתכם מכל

חטאתיכם לפני ה' תטהרו / "For this day *will* atone for you, to purify you from all your sins; before Hashem you *will* be purified" (*Vayikra*, 16:30)

This is the truth, and the feeling of joy is authentic. If by contrast we feel down, exhausted, depleted and empty after Yom Kippur, and because of that, or for other reasons, we think that maybe all that prayer was just a waste of time, or that our Teshuvah was not accepted, then we must immediately declare, "*VeHu Rachum, Yechaper Avon* — please forgive us for thinking we are not forgiven!"

MY SIN DOES NOT DEFINE ME

Our sentiments of self-worth, lightness and feeling forgiven after, or even during, Yom Kippur are not in contradiction with the wise words of King David who said, וחטאתי נגדי תמיד / "My sin is before me constantly" (*Tehilim*, 51:5). If you transgressed and then did sincere Teshuvah, certainly on the evening following Yom Kippur, if you still feel overburdened by the effects of your actions, if you still feel inadequate, unworthy, doubtful or hopeless because of what you have done, then your actions are no longer "before" you, rather they are *in* you. Even more devastating, perhaps they *are* you — the negative actions are who you are, they are defining you as a person, *Chas veShalom* / Heaven forbid.

Certainly, the past can sometimes seem overwhelmingly heavy, like an anchor that holds you down and pulls you lower and lower into an abyss. By obsessing over your past, you give it permission to keep you from living your life in the present.

Following the episode of the Golden Calf in the Desert, according to Rashi, we were told to establish and erect a Mishkan, a tabernacle, a temporary Temple as an atonement. Moshe tells the people to go gather and bring the materials to build the Mishkan, and that is what Klal Yisrael does. With tremendous *Nidvas Libam* / generosity of heart, and in a loving frenzy, the people begin to gather and assemble the materials, the gold, silver, copper, and so forth. A short time after the command, the wise artisans come to Moshe and say to him, מרבים העם להביא מדי העבדה למלאכה / "The people are bringing more than is needed for the tasks entailed in the work" (*Shemos,* 36:5). Simply, there is more than enough physical material. On a deeper level, they are saying, 'The people have done enough Teshuvah!'. Since the Mishkan comes to bring an atonement to Klal Yisrael, the wise men say it is sufficient, and they should stop. Their fiery giving, their passionate Teshuvah, if it continues any further, will move from healthy, enthusiastic regret and resolve, into obsession and imbalance.

There is a point where you must let go of perfectionism. True, you need to deal with your past, but not to the detriment of the present. There is no question that we need to fix what was broken, yet if it becomes imbalanced it can take over our life and make things even worse. Sometimes we need to "stop" being in the past and begin focusing on the present and future; we need to let go of the 'imperfect self' and simply focus on our inherent perfection. When we fail we should not give up hope and begin cultivating a feeling that we are a failure. We need to learn to cut our losses, at least for the time being, and move on. Perhaps later we will have the capacity for a more balanced and self-elevating Teshuvah.

To be forgiven means to become unburdened by the weight of your past actions; the negative past no longer blocks you from receiving the gift of the present. Again, this is not to say that you relinquish ownership of those past actions, or that you simply deny that they happened, but in your acknowledgement of those "sins", they remain "in front of me", not 'in' me. Your wrongdoings are not you, nor even attached to you; they are outside of you, in front of you. This is a level of freedom from them. It allows you to acknowledge, 'I am forgiven. I can live freely in the now.' Now you are truly empowered to change.

In fact, when your past no longer blocks you from the present, you can be sure that you *have* been forgiven. In this way, even as you acknowledge those actions as 'my problems', at the same moment you can acknowledge that you are forgiven. As you move from sins of the past to the forgiveness of the present, you truly gain the ability to change; for change can only occur in the present.

This freedom and presence is an appropriate feeling to have as Yom Kippur concludes. If we do not feel this way, but rather think that we may not have been forgiven, then we need to make Teshuvah for those thoughts and confess with all our sincerity: *VeHu Rachum, Yechaper Avon* / "And He *is* the Merciful One and *does* forgive sin..."

Among the hindrances to genuine spiritual growth, most devastating is self-doubt and *Ye'ush* / giving up hope. A person cannot take a single step forward with Ye'ush. There are those who doubt their abilities and capabilities, and there are those who even doubt themselves as a person. Sometimes this is due to past actions and a sensitive conscience and sometimes it is because of the person's upbringing. Some have learned to believe that they are basically unworthy, and some even believe that they cannot change and become 'worthy'. To rid ourselves of any trace of such destructive self-doubt, as well as doubt in the potential of the present and the future, one should realize and always remember that if Hashem, the Master of the Universe, thinks we are worth creating and worth sustaining in this moment, then we are certainly worthy and capable of change.

If we have passed though Rosh Hashanah and we are still alive, we have been judged for life. In the same way, if we have just completed Yom Kippur, we have been atoned, as Hashem says, "Today is a day of atonement." We need to really ingest and internalize this reality. If one can still somehow think, after all the fasting and praying, that perhaps one is still a sinner or a lowly person, amounting to nothing, without hope for a better future, then one must immediately Daven to the Master of the Universe, 'Please forgive me for having such thoughts! Please make me feel light and unburdened, free, open and *consciously* forgiven so I can serve You, and serve my true self and the world around me, with *Simchas haChayim* / joy of life — through *Simchas haTorah* / joy of living the Torah.

Forgiveness is experienced as a sensation of elation in releasing any negative baggage that has been weighing you down. In the times of the Beis haMikdash a person who sinned would bring an offering. Says the Zohar (*Zohar* 3, 240a), a person would know that his Teshuvah had been accepted on High when he saw an image of a lion of fire appear suspended over the Altar. Today, without a Beis haMikdash we do not have such overt indications. Yet, as the *Seforim* / holy books tell us, when we are forgiven, we feel an inner sense of relief and a joy entering us. On an intellectual level we may not 'know' whether we are forgiven or not, but the fact that there is palpable joy in the air as Yom Kippur comes to an end, is to be regarded as proof that we have *all* been forgiven. Our souls sense the cleansing and purification, and feel the lightness of having been freed of negativity, toxicity and sin.

We may not seem to hear the Heavenly Voice that says, "Go eat your bread with joy and drink your wine with a merry heart," but we do sense this message on a deeper, nonverbal level, and we should not, G-d forbid, doubt it or push it aside.

We should embrace this time of joy. And very soon, in just four short days we will be celebrating "the Season of our Rejoicing" the Yom Tov of Sukkos. Four is the number of letters in the Name of Hashem (Yud-Hei-Vav-Hei), and thus during each of these four days we are unpacking and revealing another dimension of Hashem's Name. This is the Name that we experience on Yom Kippur (*Lifnei Hashem Titaru* / "...before Yud-Hei-Vav-Hei will you be purified"). Customarily, we begin to actually build or at least speak about building our Sukkah on this very night, the evening following Yom Kippur, when the Heavenly Voice rings out and says "Go eat your bread with joy and drink your wine with a merry heart."

SUKKOS

Rosh Hashanah & Yom Kippur become Revealed

S UKKOS, IN ITS *IKAR* / ESSENCE, IS A CELEBRATION OF THE *Yetzias Mitzrayim* / Going out of Egypt, just like the other seven-day Yom Tov of the year, Pesach. Regarding Sukkos the Torah tells us, "You shall live בסכת / in *Sukkos* / booths for seven days; all citizens in Israel shall live בסכת in order that future generations ידעו / 'may know' that I made the Children of Israel live בסכות when I brought them out of the land of Egypt; I am Hashem your G-d" (*Vayikra*, 23:41-42).

What does it mean that we need to sit for seven days in a *Sukkah* / temporary hut or 'booth', so that we know that Hashem made us live in *Sukkos* when we left Egypt? What Sukkos did Hashem make us live in? And why do we need to remember them?

It seems clear that the Torah is saying that we need to remember that we sat in booths as we left Egypt, however, there are two opinions regarding what the Torah is referring to when it uses the term *Sukkos*. Rebbe Akiva says that Hashem sat them in literal booths, and we need to remember those. Rebbe Eliezer argues that "booths" refers to the Clouds of Glory — as we left Egypt we were shielded and protected by the Clouds of Glory, and we need to remember those (*Sukkah*, 11a).

WHY THIS TIME OF YEAR?

Rebbe Akiva's opinion is the straightforward reading of the *Pasuk* / verse: we need to remember that Hashem sat us in booths when we left Egypt. Obvious questions about this arise (although our sitting in a Sukkah could be a *Chok* / super-rational Mitzvah, in which case questioning it could be 'irrelevant'). First of all, why do we do this? What is so special or amazing about having sat in booths as we left Egypt; why is there an obligation to remember or commemorate this event? In fact, the booths seem inconsequential to the Exodus from Egypt — would it not be just as relevant to commemorate the type of sandals that Klal Yisrael wore when they left Egypt? Secondly, neither the miracles of the Well of Miriam nor the daily appearance of *Mon* / Manna warrant even a one day Yom Tov. Why do the booths demand a full seven day celebration?

Let us assume that the opinion of Rebbe Eliezer, that we are celebrating the miracle of the Clouds of Glory on this Yom Tov, answers the first question of 'why' we are remembering sitting in booths. It is because we are gratefully commemorating a miraculous protection and shade. But this leaves the second question unanswered: why commemorate this miracle over the other miracles in the desert? And perhaps a bigger question still applies to both opinions: we were redeemed from Egypt during the month of Nisan, which is six months before Tishrei, so why are we celebrating the booths or the Clouds of Glory in the month of Tishrei at all?

Let us begin exploring these questions with the Tur, Rav Yaakov ben Asher (c.1269 - c. 1343) who was one of the great systematic codifiers of *Halachah* / Law. He writes (*Tur, Orach Chayim*, 625) that the Yom Tov of Sukkos is actually a remembrance of the Going Out of Egypt (This is also the opinion of the Radbaz *Metzudas David,* Mitzvah 117). This answer reveals the depth of the argument of Rebbe Akiva: that we are commemorating sitting in booths as we left Egypt. It also reveals the depth of the argument of Rebbe Eliezer: that the Sukkah reminds us of the miracle of the Clouds of Glory (*Taz*, Ibid, 1:1). The purpose of the Yom Tov is to remember the Going Out of Egypt and the booths or the Clouds of Glory is a means to be reminded. For if the Mitzvah was to remember the miracle of the Clouds of Glory, why is there no Yom Tov for the other miracles in the Desert, the Mon and Well of Miriam, as the Bach notes (625:2:1)? The Mitzvah for all generations is ידעו / to know that Hashem took us out of Egypt, period. And perhaps it is only a secondary issue that when Hashem took us out of Egypt, we sat in booths and within the Clouds of Glory.

This leads us back to the question, 'Why should we celebrate Sukkos in Tishrei, and not in Nissan, if it commemorates *Yetzias*

Mitzrayim / the Going Out of Egypt?' And if Sukkos commemorates specifically the Clouds and the booths, which we surely sat in
for an extended period of time, why commemorate them in Tishrei? Continues the Tur, we celebrate Sukkos in Tishrei because if
we would move our meals and 'dwellings' into booths during Nisan, the first month of the spring, it could be perceived that we
are doing so (for recreation) like all peoples do during the spring,
and then it would not be clear to all that it is a Mitzvah. Therefore,
Hashem tells us to go out of our homes and into booths during the
seventh month, the rainy season, just when people normally move
out of their tents or gazebos and go into their permanent structures. This way, it will be clear to all that we are doing so because of
the command of the King.

Even Ezra (*Vayikra*, 23:43) writes that the reason Sukkos is placed
in Tishrei and not in Nisan, when Klal Yisrael left Egypt, is because in fact Klal Yisrael actually did not rest in physical booths
when they first left Egypt. When they first left Egypt the Clouds
of Glory protected them from the hot sun of spring through summer, and they apparently did not need any other form of protection.
But before winter began, they needed to create booths to protect
themselves from the cold, and thus we commemorate these *Sukkos*
/ booths in the month of Tishrei, before the onset of the winter.

This weather-based reason of the Even Ezra and Tur provides
an answer why Sukkos is not in the spring, but the question remains why it is specifically in Tishrei. If we sit in a Sukkah during
the rainy season to prove that we are doing so for a Mitzvah, why
not sit in the onset of winter rather than the fall? One reasonable
answer for this is that in bitter winter cold it would be too uncom-

fortable to sit in a Sukkah, and we would thus be exempt from the
Mitzvah. But why not then do it in Cheshvan? Similarly, if the issue is that Bnei Yisrael built booths *before* the winter, then perhaps
we should celebrate in Cheshvan, which is the last month before
winter.

It could be argued (at least according to the Tur) that the reason
Tishrei was chosen — as opposed to Cheshvan, for example — is
that Tishrei is the beginning of the fall rainy season, so in order to
display a contrast with the people who are moving from their ga-
zebo into their home, we move from our home out to our Sukkah;
later in the winter no one is still moving from outdoors into their
homes. Yet, fall begins in Elul*, and the true transitional month is
the following month, Cheshvan, so why not celebrate Sukkos in
Elul or Cheshvan?

Most importantly, all of this would seem a bit coincidental or
superficial if it is simply a seasonal weather pattern that pushes off
the Yom Tov of Sukkos six months, from Nissan to Tishrei. As everything can and should be understood on multiple levels, what is

---

* Although the fall months begin in Elul, it could be argued that Tishrei was
nonetheless chosen because as Chazal tell us, שילהי דקייטא קשיא מקייטא / "The
end of summer heat is more oppressive than the heat of the summer itself"
(*Yuma*, 29a), and as Rashi notes (ad loc) this refers to the month of Elul. In
this way, Tishrei is really the first cooler month of the year. And the reason
that the 15th of Tishrei was chosen, and not the first day of Tishrei, is that the
first day of the month is already a Yom Tov, Rosh Hashanah, so it needed to be
later. Additionally, since the Torah establishes things in the *middle* (see *Chazon
Ish*, Orach Chayim, Moed, 138:4), thus, the Torah establishes Sukkos in the
middle of the first cooler month, when Klal Yisrael first built their booths for
protection from the cold, and when we can move from our homes outside while
everyone else is moving indoors.

the deeper reason that Sukkos is in Tishrei? And why does Sukkos follow Yom Kippur? And why specifically does Sukkos begin on the fifteenth of the month?

FREEDOM 'FROM' & FREEDOM 'TO': THE TWO YAMIM TOVIM FOR THE EXODUS FROM EGYPT

As the Tur explains, and as is obvious from the Pesukim, Sukkos is a Yom Tov to remember *Yetzias Mitzrayim* / the Going out of Egypt — but this raises a simple, fundamental question: why should there be a Yom Tov of Sukkos at all? If the essence of Sukkos is not the booths or the Clouds of Glory, rather, a remembrance of Yetzias Mitzrayim, why should there be *two* full seven-day Yomim Tovim, Pesach and Sukkos, to remember it? Yes, there are many Mitzvos that serve as a reminder of Yetzias Mitzrayim, as the Tur himself writes, but why the need for these two specific Yomim Tovim? Why isn't Pesach sufficient as a Yom Tov to remember Yetzias Mitzrayim?

It could be argued that Pesach focuses on the most elemental level of our lives: food and nourishment, thus it remembers Yetzias Mitzrayim through eating the Pesach sacrifice, Matzah and Maror. Whereas, Sukkos is connected to the higher need of shelter, thus we celebrate our being protected and sheltered in our journey from Mitzrayim. Yet, if there are two Yomim Tovim because Yetzias Mitzrayim involves a two stage process, the two stages must be of a deeper issue than merely this hierarchy of physical needs (For example, the Rambam writes that Pesach is connected to the miracles of the Exodus whereas Sukkos is connected to the miracles in the Desert. – אמנם הדעת הדעת ב׳פסח

הזכרת 'אותות מצרים' והתמדתה לדורות; אמנם הדעת ב'סוכות' – להתמיד זכר 'אותות המדבר' לדורות (*Moreh Nevuchim*, 3:43). The fact is, genuine, lasting freedom entails two progressive levels: the negation of the negative and the assuming of the positive. In literal redemption from slavery, there is first a freeing of the slave, and then there is a stage of the slave learning to live as a free person. First comes throwing off the yoke of the master and the slave mentality, and then comes identifying with freedom, feeling free and acting free. Experiencing the first stage does not guarantee that the second stage will follow. There are plenty of examples of a slave or prisoner being physically freed, but remaining in a mindset of slavery and imprisonment. Often due to this, before long they reverted to their former physical state.

Getting rid of the negative is merely step one. Step two is assuming a new posture, actively owning freedom and living from that space. The negation of the negative only creates the context for the necessary step of attaining a positive mindset and way of living.

There is 'freedom *from*' — from oppression, slavery, and a negative situation, and there is 'freedom *to*' — to choose a new way of living, to choose postive freedom.

Normally, the movement from stage one to stage two takes time. To feel truly free demands an unlearning of an identification with oppression, and an owning of self and your life. A slave does not own his life, his master does. Owning your life means living with the recognition that you, and you alone, are responsible for your life and your happiness. Sadly, for people who had been oppressed for years, whether collectively or individually, becoming free from their oppressive situation does not necessarily mean they will begin to live freely and take responsibility for their own lives. A victim can easily become a perpetrator, *Chas veShalom* / Heaven forbid. It takes time and effort, perseverance and patience for a total rewiring of one's mindset to hold, and thus allow for the individual to live authentically and free. This is the Yom Tov of Sukkos.

Pesach and Sukkos both celebrate our collective redemption from Egypt, yet Pesach speaks more about our freedom from oppression and the birth of our nation, while Sukkos speaks of Klal Yisrael as a free and responsible people.

After Pesach, after we commemorate our freedom *from* oppression and slavery, our celebration culminates with Shavuos, the day the Torah was given to us at Mount Sinai. Yet, we were not really ready to receive it, and we needed to be 'forced', compelled to receive it: "'And they stood *under* the Mount.' Rav Avdimi…said, 'This teaches that the Holy One, blessed be He, overturned the mountain upon them like an (inverted) cask, and said to them, 'If you accept the Torah, good, and if not, here shall be your burial'" (*Shabbos*, 88a).

Matan Torah / the Giving of the Torah forced us to recieve the world of Mitzvos, reward and punishment, accountability, and responsibility for our lives. That it needed to be forced upon us shows that we were not yet ready for stage two — choosing to live as free people, without compulsion. We were freed *from* our negative circumstances in Mitzrayim, but not yet free *to* live in positive freedom. In fact, a mere 40 days after the giving of the Torah we created an idol, the Golden Calf, and many wished to go back to their old immature Egyptian habits, such as idol worship.

Creating the *Egel haZahav* / Golden Calf indicated that we did not yet absorb the message from Sinai and wished to live in a *Mitzri* / Egyptian mindset, which is interwoven with idol worship.

We regressed. We were technically free, no longer actual slaves, but we had not yet chosen real freedom, which is freedom to serve HaKadosh Baruch Hu and live a life of commitment and meaning, responsibility and integrity.

Following the episode of the Egel haZahav, Moshe comes down the mountain and sees that not only are we regressing to a pre-Matan Torah state of consciousness and behavior, but we are doing so with joy and dance, excited to let go of the Sinai revelation and experience. Moshe then smashes the Luchos upon which are engrained the essence of Torah. Some 80 days later, on the tenth of Tishrei, atonement is granted to Klal Yisrael and Moshe comes back down the Mountain for the second time, bringing to us the second set of Luchos. We are now ready to receive them and live by them, by choice.

What occurs between the smashing of the first Luchos and the giving of the second, eternally unbroken, Luchos is *Teshuvah* / returning to our purpose, taking responsibility for our actions, owning our lives, owning our mistakes and learning from them. We were able to observe our mistakes, regret them, and accept upon ourselves a different way of conduct.

Six months after leaving Egypt we finally attained the second step of freedom, the freedom to choose *Torah* / Divine Instruction, to choose a life of commitment, higher values and higher accountability.

On Pesach we are freed from oppression, slavery, addiction, and even our *Yetzer haRa* / inclination to negativity, which is our inner Egypt. We are liberated from our constrictions and limitations, as Pesach is a time of *Gadlus* / physical and spiritual expansiveness (as explored in the volume, *The Month of Nisan*).

In contrast to Pesach, on Sukkos there is no trace of remembering slavery and oppression; there is only joy. On Pesach night we eat *Maror* / bitter herbs: "This Maror that we eat for what reason? Because the Egyptians embittered our fathers in Egypt." We also eat Karpas dipped in salt water, as a reminder of our tears. We recite the Hagadah over a broken piece of "poor man's bread". This is because Pesach is about 'freedom *from*'. We remember where we came from, and how we were taken out of that state. On the night of Pesach we declare, "We were slaves to Pharaoh in Egypt, but Hashem, our G-d, brought us out from there with a strong hand and an outstretched arm", speaking of our physical freedom. We declare, "In the beginning our fathers served idols; but now the Omnipresent One has brought us close to His service," speaking of our spiritual freedom. Throughout the seven nights and days of Sukkos we mention nothing about 'slavery' or 'idol worship' or about 'bitterness' or 'tears'. We only celebrate the second dimension of Yetzias Mitzrayim, that we are a free people who freely choose the path of Torah.

On Pesach, we are spoon-fed the 'food of freedom' by our Divine Parent. That is a necessary stage. But on Sukkos, we move fearlessly and on our own power into a Sukkah, a temporary structure with very little 'Parental' protection — very little physical protection from the elements and potential intruders. In this mature level of freedom, we actively declare our freedom to be ourselves and affirm that there is nothing external that can cause us to live in fear.

Pesach celebrates our redemption from oppression; Sukkos celebrates that we are truly free. This is why Sukkos follows Yom Kippur, the day of responsibility and re-acceptance of Matan Torah. And this is why we need two full-fledged Yamim Tovim to remember Yetzias Mitzrayim.

SUKKOS FOLLOWING YOM KIPPUR: HASHEM PROTECTS US ALWAYS, EVEN AFTER WE FALL

This helps us understand why there are two Yamim Tovim and what the Yom Tov of Sukkos comes to remind us and embody. Yet a question arises: why do we need to remember Yetzias Mitzrayim specifically through a Sukkah, and not any other type of outdoor booth? There is clearly something unique about the fact that the Sukkah is a temporary structure, and that it is covered with S'chach. What is the significance of sitting in a temporary structure under the "shadow" of S'chach, and what is its relationship with the second stage of freedom?

After offering verbatim the words of the Tur, the *Aruch haShulchan* (Orach Chayim, 625:5) writes, (to paraphrase): The reason Sukkos is in Tishrei and not in Nisan is because HaKadosh Baruch Hu wants to show us that even after we have sinned and strayed from the path of righteousness, justice, Torah and Mitzvos, Hashem still protects us, and in His *Tzeil* / shadow we rest, protected under His wings. This is just like in the Desert where, following Matan

Torah (in Sivan), we sinned with the Golden Calf and then we were forgiven and given the second set of Luchos on Yom Kippur. And the next day, after Yom Kippur, we were commanded to create a *Mikdash* / a temporary Temple so that Hashem's Presence would rest there and among us. This way, the Clouds of Glory did not depart from us. Similarly, HaKadosh Baruch Hu gave us the Mitzvah of Sukkos to reenact this for all generations. Meaning, although we may have sinned through the prior year and not lived up to our full potential, nonetheless on Yom Kippur, when we align with Teshuvah we are atoned and can begin with a clean slate. As a sign that Teshuvah has been achieved, right after Yom Kippur we are commanded and invited to fashion a Sukkah, where therein we sit in the *Tzeil* / shadow and protection of HaKadosh Baruch Hu, as the verse says; "I delight to sit in his shade" (*Shir haShirim,* 2:3) which refers to Sukkos (*Zohar* 3, 255b). This shows us that even after we have sinned, strayed and done Teshuvah, Hashem's love for us is eternal and He forever watches over us and protects us from all hardship, and we even get to sit in His holy, pure Tzeil.

This idea places Sukkos within the context of the High Holy Days; the reason it follows Yom Kippur and why we sit in the Tzeil and protection of HaKadosh Baruch Hu.

The Sukkah is not merely a 'booth' or 'temporary structure' built because there is Mitzvah to build it. The Sukkah becomes an object of holiness in its own right. When we are sitting in a Sukkah we are literally sitting in Hashem's embrace, in Hashem's canopy, in the Clouds of Glory. Throughout the year, we may have drifted, and G-d forbid even overtly left the Clouds of Glory, the revealed Presence of the Shechinah. Then Rosh Hashanah comes and we awaken from our slumber. Yom Kippur comes and we are washed clean and fully atoned. Now comes Sukkos and in a revealed way we sit basking in the Presence and full embrace of HaKadosh Baruch Hu.

In a beautiful image, the Baal Shem Tov teaches that when we enter the Sukkah we are like a child running to be protected by his or her mother (*Ma'or vaShemesh*, Rimzei Yom Beis Sukkos). Just as a child who feels threatened runs to his mother and hides under her dress, we too, consciously or unconsciously, feel we are in peril because of our previous actions. Thus through doing Teshuvah we run and hide in the אימא עילאה / *Ima Ila'ah* / Supernal Divine Mother. Finally, this manifests outwardly as we enter the holy Sukkah and are protected from all negative influences, sitting under the protection of our Mother.

Similarly, we can imagine a child who, Heaven forbid, has become separated from his or her beloved parent and is lost. Or, a child 'rebels' and G-d forbid, runs away from home, and then one day the child finds his mother or desires to reconnect. In any case, this child, having lost his way, now runs back into the ever-loving embrace of his mother. On Yom Kippur we all return home, some from further distances than others, but everyone experiences a deep sense of returning home. On Sukkos we are already home and Hashem is holding us tight and near. The Shechinah embraces us in Her loving embrace and is gently telling us, 'Everything is okay, you are home. I love you, and I will forever protect you." And thus our heart soars in joy.

Whereas on Yom Kippur we turned to the Master of the Universe, and said, 'Please pick me up, I have fallen,' or 'Give me strength because I am falling,' on Sukkos we enter into the Divine hug of the Sukkah and come to the realization that there is nowhere to fall, for where ever we go we are always surrounded within Hashem's loving embrace.

WHY BEGIN SUKKOS ON THE 15ᵀᴴ OF THE MONTH?

Now we understand why Sukkos follows Yom Kippur, and why Sukkos is a full seven day Yom Tov celebrating *Yetzias Mitzrayim* / the Going Out of Egypt and the sense of being free. What still demands an explanation is why specifically does Sukkos begin on the 15th, the midpoint of the month? (Besides for the reason that the Torah always establishes constructs in the 'middle' [*Chazon Ish*, Orach Chayim, Moed, 138:4], and thus, a Yom Tov connected to a whole month would begin in the middle of the month).

When Klal Yisrael fashioned the Golden Calf, the Clouds of Glory, which had enveloped them as they left Egypt, departed (*Targum*, Shir haShirim, 2:17. Although Nechemiah, 9:18-19, says, "Even though you have made the Golden Calf...You in Your great mercy did not leave them, and the Pillar of Cloud was *not* taken away from them." This seems to suggest that even after the sin, the Clouds of Glory did not depart. But perhaps the Pasuk is talking about the clouds that guided them, but not the 'Clouds of Glory', which were there simply for the *Kavod* / glory of Klal Yisrael. It seems that the *Aruch haShulchan*, quoted above, does not quote the teaching of the Gra precisely because he brings — two halachos prior — the Pasuk in Nechemiah and thus he learns from it that the Clouds of Glory never departed. In the words of the Medrash, אלא באותה שעה לא זז מחבתן, לוה להן ענני כבוד ולא פסקו מהם המן והבאר: *Medrash Rabbah*, Bamidbar, 20:19. See also, *Sefer haKuzari*, Ma'amar 1:97). They ascended when they sinned and they returned with the beginning of the building of the *Mishkan* / temporary Temple. Atonement was granted to Klal Yisrael on the 10th of Tishrei, the day that became Yom Kippur. The following morning (*Shemos*, 35:1, Rashi), Moshe gathered Klal Yisrael and informed them about the building of the Mishkan and the need to start gathering the materials to build the Mishkan. This was on the 11th of Tishrei.

Then the Torah tells us that Klal Yisrael began bringing "free-will offerings…morning after morning" (*Shemos*, 36:3), which means they brought the materials on the 12th and the 13th of the month; "morning after morning". On the 14th, the architects of the Mishkan sorted out, weighed and organized all the materials. And thus, they began to build the Mishkan on the 15th, whereupon the presence of the Clouds of Glory returned (*Pirush haGra*, Shir haShirim, 1:4).

Whereas the original Clouds of Glory ascended from them with the worshiping of the Golden Calf, they returned following the atonement of Klal Yisrael on Yom Kippur and the giving of the second set of Luchos, and more precisely on the day they began to construct the Mishkan, which was the antidote for that sin. On the 15th of the month of Tishrei the Clouds of Glory returned. This is why we begin to celebrate Sukkos on the 15th, which is the return of the Clouds of Glory.

Now, the Clouds of Glory returned to us through our own *Te-shuvah* / return and spiritual *Avodah* / work. It was through our desire to draw closer to Hashem and let go of idol worship, that we merited Yom Kippur, that we were forgiven, and that we were given the Mitzvah to build a physical space in which Hashem's Presence would rest. The Divine Presence also rested in and among us. It was through our Avodah that the Clouds of Glory returned, and in a way, it was through our Avodah that they were 'created'.

Our Avodah drew forth the Clouds of Glory during the first year of the Exodus narrative. It drew them forth again, during the times of the Mishkan and the times of the Beis haMikdash, through our Avodah of Yom Kippur and Rosh Hashanah. And even today, the Clouds of Glory are generated through our Avodah of Yom Kippur and Rosh Hashanah.

TIMES OF THE BEIS HAMIKDASH

Once our journey through the Desert was complete, the Clouds of Glory that accompanied us through that journey departed. Yet, the Torah tells us "You shall live in Sukkos seven days…in order that future generations may know that I made the children of Israel live in Sukkos when I brought them out of the land of Egypt." According to one opinion this is a reference to the Clouds of Glory, and therefore we create a Sukkah each year and remember the Clouds of Glory. (In contrast to the Tur and the Bach, the Beis Yoseph maintains that the *Da'as* / awareness we need while sitting in the Sukkah is remembering specifically the Clouds of Glory that protected us in our journey through the Desert: Mechaber, *Orach Chayim*, 625. *Kaf haChayim*, 625:2). From a deeper perspective, while sitting in the Sukkah, we are once again, on some level, sitting in the protection of Hashem's Tzeil in the Clouds of Glory. In this way the *S'chach* / covering, the permeable 'roof' which is the *Ikar* / main element of the Sukkah, embodies the Clouds of Glory, the protection of Hashem's *Tzeil* / shadow.

In the times of the Beis haMikdash, the highest, most exalted and sacred *Avodah* / service on Yom Kippur was the *Ketores* / incense offered in the Holy of Holies. It was only once a year, on Yom Kippur, the holiest day of the year, that the *Cohen Gadol* / the High Priest, potentially the holiest person alive, entered the Holy of Holies, the holiest place on earth. The Cohen Gadol would enter, with great trepidation, with a pan of burning coals in his right hand, and in his left a ladle filled with Ketores (a blend of eleven herbs and resins). Once he entered into the Holy of Holies he would gather the Ketores into his hand and place them over the coals. When an ענן / *Anan* / Cloud of the smoke of the Ketores would fill the Holy of Holies, he would gently back out of the room.

This innermost service was performed by the Cohen Gadol in utter silence and stillness. In contrast, the services in the Beis haMikdash that were done in the Outside Courtyard were performed with many Cohanim, with a backdrop of singing Levi'im and instrumental music played by Levi'im and Yisraeilim Meychasim. There were a lot of sounds and sights; animals, smoke, blood, billowing fire and music. The service of the Ketores was a silent, private Avodah. No other living being was present when the Cohen Gadol entered the Holy of Holies. Not even angels were allowed to enter (Yerushalmi, *Yuma*, 1:5). It was only one person, alone with HaKadosh Baruch Hu. *Ketores* literally means 'bonding'. This was a deeply intense moment of truth, of bonding with Hashem, with no sounds, sights or even angels.

This Avodah literally and metaphorically produced the ענן / *Anan* / Cloud of Ketores, and this cloud of smoke is connected with the ענני הכבוד / *Ananei haKavod* / Clouds of Glory.

Through the Avodah of the Cohen Gadol in the Holy of Holies, the Cloud that rises up from that intimate, sacred space, flows upward and becomes the S'chach, the embodiment of the Clouds of Glory (Mitteler Rebbe, *Ateres Rosh*, Yom haKipurim, Chap 2. Tzemach Tzedek, *Ohr haTorah*, Sukkos, p. 1,722. Rebbe Maharash, *Hemshech veKacha*, 84). The metaphysical Anan that rises from that intimate, sacred inner space, flows upward, and four days later settles back to earth becoming the S'chach. The S'chach of the Sukkah is in this way an embodiment of the *Ananei haKavod* / Clouds of Glory in which we dwell during the seven days of Sukkos.

We sit and revel in the *Ohr* / light, the *Makifim* / surrounding, transcendent lights that have been unleashed by the intense Avodah of the holiest person, on the holiest day, in the holiest inner place.

THESE DAYS

קלקלתן תקנתן / "Their failure is their remedy" — because of the collective failure of Klal Yisrael in keeping the Beis haMikdash in existence with its physical Avodah of Ketores, every single one of us when we *Daven* / pray on Yom Kippur, and do so from the innermost recess of our soul and psyche, come to embody the Cohen Gadol. We each have the immeasurable privilege and responsibility to perform the inner Avodah of the Ketores in the spiritual Holy of Holies — on behalf of Klal Yisrael and the entire world.

As the day of Yom Kippur is unfolding, we are more and more disconnected from the externalities of this world and from our assumed identity. We squeeze and push ourselves in our prayers, we sweat in our Avodah, and we peel away more and more layers of self, until we arrive at the deepest recess of our soul. Through our perseverance and perspiration, a metaphysical vaper, an Ohr Makif / Encompassing Light, flows outward and is projected from within us, much like the smoke of the cloud of incense that arose from the actual burning of the Ketores. It is this 'perspiration', 'vaper', 'smoke' that rises from us and becomes the S'chach of the Sukkah in which we sit.

At this point we enter a private quietness, a stillness and silence of our psyche, an inner sanctum that is so deeply hidden that we may only glimpse it once a year. We enter our inner Holy of Holies as the Cohen Gadol, dressed only in brilliant white light. Layers upon layers of consciousness deeper than the ego, far beyond all the noise and effort of life, radiates our own golden magnificence, our fragrant inner holiness, our pristine purity. This part of us is perpetually and forever in a state of *Ketores* / bonding and oneness with HaKadosh Baruch Hu.

Out of this act of self-transcendence and Divine intimacy, a cloud, a Makif, fills us and projects outward, much like the silent smoke of the Ketores. This 'glory' rises from within and ascends to the Essential Divine Presence. After some timeless moments, we step back gently, and Yom Kippur comes to a conclusion. Descending gradually, we enclothe ourselves in our individual personality again, and return to our homes with jubilation to eat our bread in joy. Our Ketores continues to permeate the Heavens with a *Re'ach Nicho'ach* / pleasurable scent, for four days, corresponding to the four letters of the Transcendent Name. Then we look up to find that the Cloud of Our Glory has softly settled back down to us, now hovering lovingly over us, becoming the S'chach under which we sit, in the embrace of the Sukkah.

Just as the Teshuvah of Klal Yisrael in the Desert, which culminated on Yom Kippur, brought back the Clouds of Glory on the 15th of Tishrei, our Teshuvah on Yom Kippur creates and draws down the spiritual Clouds of Glory on the 15th of Tishrei, the first day of Sukkos. Interestingly we see this cumulative process of Teshuvah, which culminates on Yom Kippur and becomes manifest in the Clouds of Glory on Sukkos, is rooted even earlier in the Avodah on Rosh Hashanah, as we are taught that the vapor produced from the hundred sounds of the Shofar creates a cumulative meta-physical "cloud" that becomes the very S'chach we sit in on Sukkos (thus S'chach is numerically 100).

We can only feel the power of the Sukkah to the extent of the quantity and quality of Teshuvah that we accomplished, and the inward 'smoke' of the Avodah of Ketores that we generated within our inner Holy of holies, on Yom Kippur. Sukkos reveals outwardly what we accomplished inwardly on Yom Kippur. Only an individual who puts in the hard spiritual work of Yom Kippur senses the majesty of Hashem's enveloping embrace on Sukkos, and senses the reality of the Clouds of Glory. If a person doesn't sense this on Sukkos, they probably did not or could not 'burn' as much 'Ketores' on Yom Kippur. However, it is never too late — one can always do Teshuvah this very moment. One can always recreate a miniature Yom Kippur of Teshuvah and fill the Heavens with fragrance during the four days before Sukkos, and then enter the fully revealed Clouds of Glory, the Sukkah.

Sensing being enveloped in Clouds of Glory is sensing a profound joy. Our joy on Sukkos corresponds to our Avodah on Yom Kippur. The harder we have worked, the more joy we will feel.

What's more, the joy we experience on Sukkos is a 'proof' that our Teshuvah, our deep, tear soaked Avodah on Yom Kippur, has achieved its goal. Our Teshuvah was accepted on High (*Sefas Emes,* Hazinu, Tav/Reish/Samach). Now we begin life anew, with wonder, freshness and overflowing happiness. Now we can joyfully draw waters from our inner wells of salvation.

ALL OF THE FIRST HALF OF TISHREI
IS REVEALED IN SUKKOS

The Radbaz (Rabbi David ben Zimra, c.1479-1573) explains that there is significance to the fact that Sukkos begins on the 15th of the month, when the moon is full (*Metzudas David,* Mitzvah 117). A full moon is a full revealing of everything that has transpired during the first 14 days. Whereas the first 14 days of the month are a time of concealed and inward illumination, on the full moon, Sukkos is an outward-moving revelation of everything that has occurred inwardly.

Rosh Hashanah begins on the first day of the month when the moon is almost totally concealed from sight. The verse says "Blow a Shofar at the New Moon, בכסה / at the 'covered' time, for our Festival day" (*Tehillim,* 81:4). "What is a Festival Day in which the moon is covered? This is Rosh Hashanah" (*Rosh Hashanah,* 8a-8b). Similarly, Yom Kippur is on the 10th of the month, when the moon is not yet fully revealed. This is because the Avodah of Rosh Hashanah, the "Ten Days of Teshuvah" and Yom Kippur are all "covered" and hidden in subtle, deep and introspective inner work. But then comes the Yom Tov of Sukkos, when we go out of the house and out of the Shul, and into the more open space of the Sukkah. Here, instead of the Avodah being one of seriousness and subtlety, the Avodah is one of externally expressed joy and even dancing.

On Sukkos, the joy we experience, the *Ohr* / light, and *Shefa* / flow that we feel, is an extension of the inner, reflective, more private Avodah we have achieved over the course of the first 14 days of Tishrei.

THE 'VAPOR' OF THE SHOFAR
CREATES THE CLOUDS OF THE S'CHACH

As we have explored, the S'chach is produced by our inner Ketores of Yom Kippur. It can also be traced back to having origins in the main Avodah of Rosh Hashanah, blowing the Shofar. The Arizal teaches that the 100 blasts of the Shofar on Rosh Hashanah are projected outward and become the S'chach of the Sukkah. The word סכך / S'chach has a numerical value of 100 (Samach/60, Chaf/20, Final Chaf/20 = 100) (*Pri Eitz Chayim*, Sha'ar haSukkos. See also, *Toras Levi Yitzchak*, p. 303), corresponding to the 100 Shofar blasts.

When we blow the Shofar, heat and moisture is projected through the breath of our mouths, coming from deep within our bodies. This 'vapor' is released into the ether, until it cumulates and forms a metaphysical cloud. This cloud is what eventually becomes the S'chach that we sit under on Sukkos.

MAKIF INTO PENIMI

On Rosh Hashanah, even on Yom Kippur and the days in between, we are doing the Avodah on a more inward level, as explored earlier. Hence, more *Ohr Makif* / general light or *Makifim* / surrounding lights — 'clouds' — are being produced. These Makifim become the S'chach of Sukkos.

On Sukkos we sit under these Makifim, yet we do so in the context of a defined, detailed, specific (meaning *Penimi* / within-the-physical-world) structure, the Sukkah. On Rosh Hashanah and Yom Kippur, the 'Makifim' we create are a general desire to live our lives with the Presence of HaKadosh Baruch Hu at all times. We declare our love for Hashem, but this is very general and intangible, and thus it generates Makifim, the surrounding Ohr of the S'chach of the Sukkah. Yet, the Sukkah itself, the walls, are a meticulously measured and defined structure. This is the *Kli* / vessel that receives the Makifim. The well-defined Sukkah is like a person who says 'I love you,' and then draws a line in the sand and says, 'and this is where I am sitting.' We tell HaKadosh Baruch Hu, 'I am here, and I am not going anywhere; I just want to be with You.' And Hashem stretches out His arms as 'the Higher Mother', and says, 'My child, I'm so glad you're here; I just want to hold you tight'.

During Rosh Hashanah and Yom Kippur we say, 'I love you Hashem,' while sitting under the Sukkah we say, 'I am now ready to live with You right here, under one roof, and spend time together, without distractions.' Hashem responds, 'Thank you, my child; yes, let these lines, these walls be our sacred space, the place where we internalize our commitment.'

And then comes an even deeper, more integrated level of drawing Makifim into Penimi, and that is with the waving of the Lulav and Esrog. On the morning of the first day of Sukkos and thereafter, we recite a blessing on the *Arba Minim* / Four Species (the *Lulav* / palm branch, two *Aravos* / willows, three or more *Hadasim* / myrtles, and an *Esrog* / citron). This is preferably performed in the Sukkah itself. Noticeably, there are three lines, three upright types of branches that we take in our right hand, and we attach and tie them as one bundle, one line. Then we take the Esrog, shaped as a 'circle', and draw all four species together. There are many symbols encoded in this Mitzvah (as explored in the book, *The Four Species: The Symbolism of the Lulav & Esrog and Intentions for the Lulav Movements*). On a simple level, the 'line' of the upright species is like an antenna that draws Light down from the S'chach, the Makifim, and then conducts this Light through the 'masculine' line further down into the 'feminine' Esrog. The Arba Minim are lifted and then waved in the four directions, as well as, up and down, and then brought back to the place of the heart. These movements push away negative distortions of the Light in the six directions, and draw downwards and inwards into the Penimi all the pure Makifim that were created from our individual and collective Avodah on Rosh Hashanah and Yom Kippur.

All in all, Sukkos is the summation and full revelation of all the effects of the effortful and emotional Avodah of Rosh Hashanah through Yom Kippur. Because these effects are *revealed*, they manifest on Sukkos as an Avodah of *Simchah* / joy. Over the course of this Avodah of joy, the Makifim that were generated from our inner work on the High Holy Days are revealed and integrated in ourselves and in the world, in a real, defined, practical way. Then we are able to take this illumination into the new year, and begin living life on a higher, deeper level than ever before.

Rebbe Zusha of Anipoli once appeared in a dream to one of his students and said; the word סוכה / *Sukkah* is an acronym for ויאמר ה' סלחתי כדברך / "And Hashem said (to Moshe), 'I have pardoned, according to your words (of request)" (*Bamidbar*, 14:2). Sukkos is the culmination and the confirmation of Yom Kippur; our Teshuvah has been accepted, as well as our request to live on a higher and deeper level this coming year.

Numerically, the word *Sukkah* is 91, which is also the value of the word אמן / *Amen* (and *Hashem* / 26 and *Ado-noi* / 65 = 91). Sukkos is thus the confirmation, the אמן / *Amein*, of all our Avodah and experiences throughout the Days of Awe. It is the focal point where we draw all of that down and 'gather' it together. From this place of 'ingathering', we can then *Daven* / pray very powerfully and confidently that HaKadosh Baruch Hu will give us and all of Klal Yisrael a *Shanah Tovah uMesukah,* a happy, healthy and sweet New Year.

OTHER BOOKS BY THE AUTHOR

RECLAIMING THE SELF
The Way of Teshuvah

Teshuvah is one of the great gifts of life. It speaks of a hope for a better today and empowers us to choose a brighter tomorrow. But what exactly is Teshuvah? How does it work? How can we undo our past and how do we deal with guilt? And what is healthy regret without eroding our self-esteem? In this fascinating and empowering book, the path for genuine transformation and a way to include all of our past in the powerful moment of the now, is explored and demonstrated.

THE MYSTERY OF KADDISH
Understanding the Mourner's Kaddish

The Mystery of Kaddish is an in-depth exploration into the Mourner's Prayer. Throughout Jewish history, there have been many rites and rituals associated with loss and mourning, yet none have prevailed quite like the Mourner's Kaddish Prayer, which has become the definitive ritual of mourning. The book explores the source of this prayer and deconstructs the meaning to better understand the grieving process and how the Kaddish prayer supports and uplifts the bereaved through their own personal journey to healing.

UPSHERNISH: The First Haircut
Exploring the Laws, Customs & Meanings of a Boy's First Haircut

What is the meaning of Upsherin, the traditional celebration of a boy's first haircut at the age of three? Why is a boy's hair allowed to grow freely for his first three years? What is the deeper import of hair in all its lengths and varieties? What is the meaning of hair coverings? Includes a guide to conducting an Upsherin ceremony.

A BOND FOR ETERNITY
Understanding the Bris Milah

What is the Bris Milah – the covenant of circumcision? What does it represent, symbolize and signify? This book provides an in depth and sensitive review of this fundamental Mitzvah. In this little masterpiece of wisdom – profound yet accessible —the deeper meaning of this essential rite of passage and its eternal link to the Jewish people, is revealed and explored.

———

REINCARNATION AND JUDAISM
The Journey of the Soul

A fascinating analysis of the concept of Gilgul / Reincarnation. Dipping into the fountain of ancient wisdom and modern understanding, this book addresses and answers such basic questions as: What is reincarnation? Why does it occur? And how does it affect us personally?

———

INNER RHYTHMS
The Kabbalah of MUSIC

Exploring the inner dimension of sound and music, and particularly, how music permeates all aspects of life. The topics range from Deveikus/Unity and Yichudim/Unifications, to the more personal issues, such as Simcha/Happiness and Marirus/ sadness.

———

MEDITATION AND JUDAISM
Exploring the Jewish Meditative Paths

A comprehensive work encompassing the entire spectrum of Jewish thought, from the sages of the Talmud and the early Kabbalists to the modern philosophers and Chassidic masters. This book is both a scholarly, in-depth study of meditative practices, and a practical, easy to follow guide for any person interested in meditating the Jewish way.

TOWARD THE INFINITE

A book focusing exclusively on the Chassidic approach to meditation known as Hisbonenus. Encompassing the entire meditative experience, it takes the reader on a comprehensive and engaging journey through this unique practice. The book explores the various states of consciousness that a person encounters in the course of the meditation, beginning at a level of extreme self-awareness and concluding with a state of total non-awareness.

THIRTY – TWO GATES OF WISDOM
into the Heart of Kabbalah & Chassidus

What is Kabbalah? And what are the differences between the theoretical, meditative, magical and personal Kabbalistic teachings? What are the four paths of interpreting the teachings of the ARIzal? What did Chassidus teach? These are some of the fundamental issues expanded upon in this text. And then, more specifically, why are there so many names of G-d and what do they represent? What are the key concepts of these deeper teachings?

The book explores the grand narrative of the great chain of reality, how there was and is a movement from the Infinite Oneness of Hashem to a world of (apparent) duality and multiplicity.

THE PURIM READER
The Holiday of Purim Explored

With a Persian name, a masquerade dress code and a woman as the heroine, Purim is certainly unusual amongst the Jewish holidays. Most people are very familiar with the costumes, Megilah and revelry, but are mystified by their significance. This book offers a glimpse into the hidden world of Purim, uncovering these mysteries and offering a deeper understanding of this unique holiday.

EIGHT LIGHTS
8 Meditations for Chanukah

What is the meaning and message of Chanukah? What is the spiritual significance of the Lights of the Menorah? What are the Lights telling us? What is the deeper dimension of the Dreidel? Rav Pinson, with his trademark deep learning and spiritual sensitivity guides us through eight meditations relating to the Lights of the Menorah, the eight days of Chanukah, and a fascinating exploration of the symbolism and structure of the Dreidel. Includes a detailed how-to guide for lighting the Chanukah Menorah.

THE IYYUN HAGADAH
An Introduction to the Haggadah

In this beautifully written introduction to Passover and the Haggadah, we are guided through the major themes of Passover and the Seder night. This slim text, addresses the important questions, such as: What is the big deal of Chametz? What are we trying to achieve through conducting a Seder? What's with all that stuff on the Seder Plate? And most importantly, how is this all related to freedom?

PASSPORT TO KABBALAH
A Journey of Inner Transformation

Life is a journey full of ups and downs, inside-outs, and unexpected detours. There are times when we think we know exactly where we want to be headed, and other times when we are so lost we don't even know where we are. This slim book provides readers with a passport of sorts to help them through any obstacles along their path of self-refinement, reflection, and self-transformation.

THE FOUR SPECIES
The Symbolism of the Lulav & Esrog

The Four Species have inspired countless commentaries and traditions and intrigued scholars and mystics alike. In this little masterpiece of wisdom both profound and practical - the deep symbolic roots and nature of the Four Species are explored. The Na'anuim, or ritual of the Lulav movement, is meticulously detailed and Kavanos,, are offered for use with the practice. Includes an illustrated guide to the Lulav Movements.

THE BOOK OF LIFE AFTER LIFE

What is a soul? What happens to us after we physically die?

What is consciousness, and can it survive without a physical brain?

Can we remember our past lives?

Do near-death experiences prove immortality?

What is Gan Eden? Resurrection?

Exploring the possibility of surviving death, the near-death experience and a glimpse into what awaits us after this life.

(This book is an updated and expanded version of the book; Jewish Wisdom of the Afterlife)

THE GARDEN OF PARADOX:
The Essence of Non – Dual Kabbalah

This book is a Primer on the Essential Philosophy of Kabbalah presented as a series of 3 conversations, revealing the mysteries of Creator, Creation and Consciousness. With three representational students, embodying respectively, the philosopher, the activist and the mystic, the book, tackles the larger questions of life. Who is G-d? Who am I? Why do I exist? What is my purpose in this life? Written in clear and concise prose, the text, gently guides the reader towards making sense of life's paradoxes and living meaningfully.

BREATHING & QUIETING THE MIND

Achieving a sense of self-mastery and inner freedom demands that we gain a measure of hegemony over our thoughts. We learn to choose out thoughts so that we are not at the mercy of whatever belches up to the mind. Through quieting the mind and conscious breathing we can slow the onrush of anxious, scattered thinking and come to a deeper awareness of the interconnectedness of all of life.

Source texts are included in translation, with how-to-guides for the various practices.

VISUALIZATION AND IMAGERY:
Harnessing the Power of our Mind's Eye

We assume that what we see with our eyes is absolute. Yet, beyond our ability to choose what we see, we have the ability to choose how we see. This directly translates into how we experience life. In a world saturated with visual imagery, our senses are continuously assaulted with Kelipa/empty/fantasy imagery that we would not necessarily choose. These images can negatively affect our relationship with ourselves, with the world around us, and with the Divine. This volume seeks to show us how we can alter that which we observe through harnessing the power of our mind's eye, the inner sanctum of our imagination. We thus create a new way to see and experience the world. This book teaches us how to utilize visualization and imagery as a way to develop our spiritual sensitivity and higher intuition, and ultimately achieve Deveikus/Unity with Hashem.

SOUND AND VIBRATION:
Tuning into the Echoes of Creation

Through our perception of sound and vibration we internalize the world around us. What we hear, and how we process that hearing, has a profound impact on how we experience life. What we hear can empower us or harm us. A defining human capacity is to harness the power sound -- through speech, dialogue, and song, and through listening to others. Hearing is primary dimension of our existence. In fact, as a fetus our ears were the first fully operating sensory organs to develop.

This book will guide you in methods of utilizing the power of sound and vibration to heal and maintain mental, emotional and spiritual health, to fine-tune your Midos and even to guide you into deeper levels of Deveikus / conscious unity with Hashem. The vibratory patterns of the Aleph-Beis are particularly useful portals into our deeper conscious selves. Through chanting and deep listening, we can use the letters and sounds to shift our very mindset, to induce us into a state of presence and spiritual elevation.

THE POWER OF CHOICE:
A Practical Guide to Conscious Living

It is the essential premise of this book that we hold the key to unlock many of the gates that seem closed to us and keep us from living our fullest life. That key we all hold is the power to choose. The Power of Choice is the primary tool that we have at our disposal to impact the world and effect change within our own lives. We often give up this power to outside forces such as the market, media, politicians or peer pressure; or to internal forces that often function beyond our conscious control such as ego, anger, lust, greed or jealousy. Making conscious, compassionate and creative decisions is the cornerstone of living a mature and meaningful life.

MYSTIC TALES FROM THE EMEK HAMELECH

Mystic Tales of the Emek HaMelech, is a wondrous and inspiring collection of stories culled from the Emek HaMelech. Emek HaMelech, from which these stories have been taken, (as well as its author) is a bit of a mystery. But like all good mysteries, it is one worth investigating. In this spirit the present volume is being offered to the general public in the merit and memory of its saintly author, as well as in the hopes of introducing a vital voice of deeper Torah teaching and tradition to a contemporary English speaking audience

---

INNER WORLDS OF JEWISH PRAYER
A Guide to Develop and Deepen the Prayer Experience

While much attention has been paid to the poetry, history, theology and contextual meaning of the prayers, the intention of this work is to provide a guide to finding meaning and effecting transformation through the prayer experience itself.

Explore: *What happens when we pray? *How do we enter the mind-state of prayer? *Learning to incorporate the body into the prayers. *Discover techniques to enhance and deepen prayer and make it a transformative experience.

This empowering and inspiring text, demonstrates how through proper mindset, preparation and dedication, the experience of prayer can be deeply transformative and ultimately, life-altering.

_____

WRAPPED IN MAJESTY
Tefillin - Exploring the Mystery

Tefillin, the black boxes and leather straps that are worn during prayer, are curiously powerful and mysterious. Within the inky black boxes lie untold secrets. In this profound, passionate and thought-provoking text, the multi-dimensional perspectives of Tefillin are explored and revealed. Magically weaving together all levels of Torah including the Peshat (literal observation), to Remez (allegorical), to Derush, (homiletic), to Sod (hidden) into one beautiful tapestry. Inspirational and instructive, Wrapped in Majesty: Tefillin, will make putting on the Tefillin more meaningful and inspiring.

_____

THE MYSTERY OF SHABBOS
Shabbat rediscovered

In THE MYSTERY OF SHABBOS, Rav Pinson delves into the transformative power of Shabbos.

With an all-encompassing perspective that ranges from the literal, Pshat observation and Halachic implications of the texts, to the allegorical, the philosophical, and finally, to the deeper secrets as revealed by Kabbalah and Chassidus, creating an elegant tapestry of thought and experience.

THE MYSTERY OF SHABBOS is a profound meditation on the meaning of Shabbos and demonstrates the physical, emotional, mental and spiritual possibilities available and given to us with the gift of Shabbos.

Studying and contemplating this inspired text on the depths of Shabbos will unveil a redemptive light in your experience of the Seventh Day — and by extension, every day of your life.

————————

SECRETS OF THE MIKVAH:
Waters of Transformation

A Mikvah is a pool of water used for the purpose of ritual immersion; a place where one moves from a state of Tumah; impurity, blockage and death— to a place of Teharah; purity, fluidity and life.

In SECRETS OF THE MIKVAH, Rav Pinson delves into the transformative powers of the Mikvah with his trademark all-encompassing perspective that ranges from the literal, Pshat observation and Halachic implications of the texts, to the allegorical, the philosophical, and finally, to the deep secrets of the Mikvah as revealed by Kabbalah and Chassidus.

This insightful and inspirational text demonstrates how immersion in a Mikvah can be a transformative and life-altering practice, and includes various Kavanos—deep intentions—for all people, through various stages of life, that empower and enrich the immersion experience.

————————

THE SPIRAL OF TIME:
A 12 Part Series on the Months of the Year.
The following titles from the series are now available!

THE SPIRAL OF TIME:
Unraveling the Yearly Cycle

Many centuries ago, the Sages of Israel were the foremost authority in the fields of both astronomical calculation and astrological wisdom, including the deeper interpretations of the cycles and seasons. Over time, this wisdom became hidden within the esoteric teachings of the Torah, and as a result was known only to students and scholars of the deepest depths of the tradition. More recently, the great teachers, from R.Yitzchak Luria (the Arizal) to the Baal Shem Tov, taught that as the world approaches the Era of Redemption, it is a Mitzvah / spiritual obligation to broadly reveal this wisdom.

"The Spiral of Time" is volume 1 is a series of 12 books, and serves as an introductory book to the basic concepts and nature of the Hebrew calendar and explores the special day of Rosh Chodesh.

————

THE MONTH OF SHEVAT:
Elevating Eating & The Holiday of Tu b'Shevat

Each month of the year radiates with a distinct Divine energy and thus unique opportunities for growth, *Tikkun* and illumination. According to the deeper teachings of the Torah, all of these distinct qualities, opportunities and natural phenomena correspond to a certain data set. That is, the nature of each month is elucidated by a specific letter of the Aleph Beis, a tribe, verse, human sense, and so forth. The month of Shevat is particularly connected to food and our relationship to bodily intake. During this month we celebrate Tu b'Shevat, the New Year of the Tree, and aspire to create a proper and physically/emotionally/spiritually healthy relationship with food.

THE MONTH OF ADAR:
Transformation Through Laughter & Holy Doubt

Each month of the year radiates with distinct Divine qualities and unique opportunities for growth and spiritual illumination. As Adar concludes the monthly cycle of the year, as well as the solar phenomena of the winter, it is an appropriate month to think about our essential identity, before moving out to meet the world come spring. This month we strive to create a healthy relationship with holy humor, unbounded joy, and a general sense of lightness of being. Through the work of Adar we transform negative, crippling doubt and uncertainties into radical wonderment and openness.

———————

THE MONTH OF IYYAR:
Evolving the Self & The Holiday of Lag b'Omer

The month of IYYAR is the second month of the spring, a month that connects the Redemption from Egypt in Nissan with the Revelation of Torah in Sivan. The Chai/ Eighteenth day of the Month is the day we celebrate the Rashbi (Rabbi Shimon Bar Yochai) and the revealing of the hidden aspects of the Torah. This is the 'Holiday' of Lag b'Omer. The book explores the unique quality of this special month, a month that has a Mitzvah of counting the Omer every day. In addition, the book explores the roots and significance of the mystical 'holiday' of Lag b'Omer. Including the customs & Practices of Lag b'Omer, such as, bonfires, bows & arrows, parades, Upsherin, and more.

———————

THE MONTH OF SIVAN
The Art of Receiving – Shavuot and Matan Torah

Each month of the year radiates with a distinct quality and provides unique opportunities for personal growth and illumination.

Sivan is the third month of the lunar cycle. One is a singularity. Two is division. Three is harmony, a unity that synthesizes individuality and multiplicity, Heaven and Earth, Spirituality and Physicality. During this month we celebrate Shavuos and the giving of the Torah, the ultimate expression of the unity of the Above and Below and we aspire to connect with the Keser/Crown of Torah that Transcends and yet includes all Worlds.

Learning how to truly receive Higher wisdom in our Lower faculties is the mental, emotional, and spiritual exercise of the month.

THE MONTHS OF TAMUZ AND AV:
Embracing Brokenness –
17th of Tamuz, Tisha B'Av, & Tu B'Av

Each month and season of the year, radiates with distinct Divine qualities and unique opportunities for growth and Tikkun.

The summer month of Tamuz and Av contain the longest and hottest days of the year. The raised temperature is indicative of a corresponding spiritual heat, a time of harsher judgement and potential destruction, such as the destructions of the first and second Beis HaMikdash, which began on the 17th of Tamuz and culminated on the 9th and 10th of Av.

A few days later, on Tu b'Av, the darkness is transformed and reveals the greatest light and possibility for new life. During these summer months of Tamuz and Av we embrace our brokenness so that we can heal and transform darkness into light.

THE MONTH OF ELUL:
Days of Introspection and Transformation

Each month of the year radiates with a distinct quality and provides unique opportunities for growth and personal transformation. Elul, as the final month of the spring/summer season is connected to endings. Elul gives us the strength to be able to finish strong, to end well. Elul also serves as a month of preparation for the New Year/Rosh Hashanah.

We inhale our past year, ending with wisdom and then we also gain the wisdom to begin anew and exhale a positive year into being. The mental, emotional, and spiritual objective of this month is introspection and the reclaiming of our inner purity and wholeness.

THE MONTH OF CHESHVAN:
Navigating Transitions, Elevating the Fall

Directly on the heels of the inspiring and holiday-filled month of Tishrei, Cheshvan is a month that is quiet and devoid of holidays. In the month of Cheshvan we use the stored up energies of the previous months to self-generate our inspiration and creativity and provide ourselves with the strength to rise up after a fall. In Cheshvan we are entering into a stormier, wetter and colder season. It is a month of transition. The mental, emotional and spiritual objective of this month is to weather the transitions, learn to self-generate and stand tall. And if we do fall, we use the quality of this month to get back up and do so with more conviction, strength, wisdom and clarity.

THE MONTH OF TEVES:
Refining Relationships, Elevating the Body

The quality of Teves is generally harsh—much like its counterpart Tamuz in the summer, thus the tendency for many is to hunker down, retract, curl up and wait for the month to pass by, only to reemerge when the harshness has dissipated. Think for a moment about the 'easier' months of the year, which, like gentle waves in the ocean, carry us where we want to go. We can ride these energies easily and they can propel us forward effortlessly, we just need to go with the overall flow, so to speak. The harsher months, on the other hand, can be compared to the more powerful waves that emanate from the belly of the ocean, which come forcefully crashing down and can easily drown a person before they even realize what has happened. However, those who want to utilize the momentum of the powerful energy that is available during such times can, with caution and creativity, harness these intense waves and ride them higher and farther than other, more gentle circumstances may allow. However, harnessing the power of Tohu, the raw energy of the body, does in fact need to be approached with great care and attention.

THE JEWISH WEDDING:
A Guide to the Rituals and Traditions of the Wedding Ceremony

This guide is based on the teachings of Torah, Talmud, Medrash, Zohar, Halacha, Poskim, Kabbalah and Chassidus. By quoting these teachings, we actively draw down the 'presence' of these holy souls who revealed these teachings, thus extending blessings to the bride and groom and all in attendance at the Chupa.